The Writer's Handbook
Guide to Writing for Children

Barry Turner has worked on both sides of publishing, as an editor and marketing director and as an author. He started his career as a journalist with *The Observer* before moving on to television and radio. He has written over twenty books including *A Place in the Country*, which inspired a television series, and a bestselling biography of the actor Richard Burton.

His recent work includes a radio play, travel articles, serialising books for *The Times*, editing the magazine *Country* and writing a one-man show based on the life of the legendary theatre critic, James Agate. Barry has just published *Countdown to Victory*, a book about the last months of World War II. He has been editor of *The Writer's Handbook* for eighteen years, and editor of *The Statesman's Yearbook* for seven.

Also edited by Barry Turner
in *The Writer's Handbook* series

The Writer's Handbook Guide to Travel Writing

From newspaper features to armchair travellers' memoirs, this highly informative guide offers all the essential information needed by any budding travel writer looking to break into this increasingly popular genre.

The Writer's Handbook Guide to Crime Writing

Drawing on a wide range of expertise, including top crime writers, agents, publishers and booksellers, this book looks at how to write a successful crime novel and get it published.

The Writer's Handbook Guide to Writing for Stage and Screen

There are increasing opportunities for new writers of plays, be it for stage, screen or radio – but also increasing demands. This highly practical and informative book looks at how to get started, and how to become a successful playwright in any area.

The Writer's Handbook 2005

The eighteenth edition of the bestselling guide to all markets for creative writing. Completely revised and updated, this is an indispensable companion for everyone in the writing profession. Offering a cornucopia of advice, information, contacts, hints and discussion, this practical, straightforward guide provides full details on the key markets.

The Writer's Handbook
Guide to Writing for Children

edited by

BARRY TURNER

MACMILLAN

First published 2004 by Macmillan
an imprint of Pan Macmillan Ltd
Pan Macmillan, 20 New Wharf Road, London N1 9RR
Basingstoke and Oxford
Associated companies throughout the world
www.panmacmillan.com

ISBN 1 4050 0101 1

Contents

LISTINGS

A View from the Top

*Talking to Barry Turner, Philip Pullman points
the way for the new wave of children's writers*

BARRY TURNER: In your article for *The Writer's Handbook* in 2000 you suggested that children's fiction was patronised by general publishing. Is this still true?

PHILIP PULLMAN: Not so much. The scene has changed – more, I suspect, because some children's books have made large amounts of money than because literary editors have suddenly become aware of quality they were somehow unable to see before.

BT: How far is inspiration a factor in the business of writing?

PP: Less than non-writers think. If you're going to make a living at this business – more importantly, if you're going to write anything that will last – you have to realise that a lot of the time, you're going to be writing without inspiration. The trick is to write just as well without it as with. Of course, you write less readily and fluently without it; but the interesting thing is to look at the private journals and letters of great writers and see how much of the time they just had to do without inspiration. Conrad, for example, groaned at the desperate emptiness of the pages he faced; and yet he managed to cover them. Amateurs think that if they were inspired all the time,

1

they could be professionals. Professionals know that if they relied on inspiration, they'd be amateurs.

BT: What, if any, are the advantages for the author in having a young readership?

PP: It forces you not to let the story go out of your mind. If you stop telling a story, they stop reading. Story is very important; it's the events themselves, as Isaac Bashevis Singer says, that contain the wisdom – not what we say about them.

BT: When you begin a book, does the plot come first or do you construct the story around characters that already exist in your mind? Or perhaps you begin from an entirely different point?

PP: I begin with a picture of something intriguing happening, and I write to find out what led up to it and what the outcome will be. But everyone is different; this is what works for me.

BT: At what stage do you have your plot fully worked out?

PP: Just after the book is published, at the point when it's too late to fix all the problems.

BT: Where do you go to look for your characters? Are they ever based on people you know?

PP: I don't look for them. It feels as if they look for me, and they come fully formed. I seldom if ever have to make conscious adjustments. Mind you, I often have to wait quite a long time.

BT: You have written several series with recurring characters. Do you set out with that intention and, if not, at what stage is it apparent that the characters have the scope to develop over several titles?

PP: I become fond of a character and see that there's another story in them – that's what usually happens. Besides, if I've already made up the background and done the reading and so on, I don't want to waste that work.

BT: Your daily regime of hand-writing three pages every day in the shed at the bottom of your garden is well documented and you have previously stressed the importance of a disciplined approach to writing. Did you manage to stick to a rigorous schedule even before you were able to devote your whole time to writing?

PP: It was easier then. The work of being a schoolteacher (for instance) is regular and timetabled, and you can build in your writing to the hour or so after midnight or before breakfast or whenever. But when you work full-time, the demands on your attention come flying from every direction and unpredictably, and it's harder to find that regularity that is so necessary.

BT: Do you edit and re-write as you go along or do you wait until you have a complete draft?

PP: Both.

BT: You have been quoted as saying writer's block is 'howling nonsense'. But do you have any tricks to help things along when the words are not coming out as you want them to?

PP: No tricks. I just sit there groaning.

BT: Do you test out your stories on anyone while you're writing them?

PP: Never. My stories are none of the readers' business until I have finished them. The idea of asking people what they think is so bizarre as to be inconceivable to me; if these people know how a story should go, why aren't they writing stories of their own? I am a strong believer in the tyranny, the dictatorship, the absolute authority of the writer. On the other hand, when it comes to reading, the only thing that works is democracy.

BT: The success of the *His Dark Materials* trilogy, the Harry Potter books and the renewed interest in J.R.R. Tolkien has seen fantasy dominate the children's market in recent years. Do you think it's important for aspiring children's writers to keep in mind current trends or should they forget such considerations?

PP: What they should do is take no notice whatsoever, and write exactly what they want to write. Back in 1996, how many people did we hear saying 'We want the first Harry Potter book! We wish someone would write a book about Harry Potter! When is the first Harry Potter book going to come out? We can't wait!' None, is the answer. It's silly to ask the public what it wants. The public doesn't know what it wants until it sees what you can offer. So follow the whole of your nature and write the book that only you can write, and see what happens.

BT: Did you or your publisher have any inclination of how success-ful the *His Dark Materials* trilogy would be when you first came up with the idea?

PP: Absolutely none. I thought it would be read by about 500 people at most. But it was a book I wanted to write, and David Fickling wanted to publish.

BT: Your books deal with many of life's big questions: God, the

4

Church, good and evil, love; and you are not afraid to challenge your young readers. Is that a conscious aim when you sit down in front of a blank sheet of paper? Do you think children's writing has a duty to pose difficult questions?

PP: No. The duty it has is best expressed in the words of Dr Johnson: 'The only aim of writing is to help the reader better to enjoy life, or better to endure it.'

BT: You have run into criticism from certain religious groups who regard you as subversive, with the *Catholic Herald* describing your work as 'worthy of the bonfire'. Do such emotional responses concern or upset you or does it please you to generate strong reactions?

PP: I'm delighted to have brought such excitement into what must be very dull lives.

BT: *Northern Lights* was re-titled *The Golden Compass* for the American market. Why did this change come about? Do you have a title in mind when you start a story?

PP: Sometimes I do, sometimes I don't. The editor who made that change was also responsible for changing *Harry Potter and the Philosopher's Stone*, which made sense, into *Harry Potter and the Sorcerer's Stone*, which didn't. At the time, I didn't have enough clout to resist.

BT: You were a fan of comic books from childhood and your own stories are filled with striking imagery. Do you see your subject matter visually as you write?

PP: Yes. I like to make various things clear: where a scene is taking place, what time of day it is, where the light's coming from, what the weather's like, who's present – that sort of thing. Not all of them all the time, but some of them most of the time. It helps the reader to see what you would like them to see.

BT: Have you consciously set out to create female heroines like Lyra and Sally Lockhart? Have you found any difficulties as a male writer in creating young female characters?

PP: No. I write almost always in the third person, and I don't think the narrator is male or female anyway. They're both, and young and old, and wise and silly, and sceptical and credulous, and innocent and experienced, all at once. Narrators are not even human – they're sprites. So there are no limits, no areas, or characters, or sexes, or times, where these sprites can't go. And they fix on what interests them. I wouldn't dream of deliberately choosing this or that sort of person, for political or social or commercial reasons, to write a book about. If the narrator isn't interesting, the book won't come alive.

BT: Your work has been performed on radio, television and the stage, and the film rights to *His Dark Materials* have been sold. Is it difficult to give up your work to someone else's interpretation?

PP: No. The democracy of reading means that as soon as a book is published you lose control of how it's interpreted anyhow, and so you should. To tell someone else how to read your book is to fall into the temptation of fundamentalism. When it comes to performance and film and so on, what you should do, it seems to me, is make sure the people you sell it to know what they're doing, and then leave them alone. You are better employed writing new books than arguing with people about how to interpret your existing ones.

BT: Have you had any involvement in casting characters? Do you have preconceived notions of what they should be like?

PP: I do have ideas, and when it's useful I make suggestions. But professional theatre or film people know far more actors and have far more knowledge than I have.

BT: Can aspiring writers learn much from creative writing courses?

PP: Goodness knows. I don't think they would have helped me much. The most useful quality you can have as a writer (given a basic amount of talent) is stubbornness, pig-headedness, call it what you will – the insistence against all the evidence that you will produce something worth reading. I'm not sure you can teach that.

BT: With publishers aware of the astronomical sales now possible, is this good news for emerging writers or does it generate pressures from publishers to clone a new 'Lyra and Will' or 'Harry Potter'?

PP: Publishers always want to publish what was a hit last year. Great publishers have the courage and vision to back things that might be successful in the future, but about which no one can be sure.

BT: For somebody looking to get their stories for children published, is there any single piece of advice you would offer them?

PP: Write exactly what only you can write. Don't make commercial calculations. Be crazy about it. Insist on the primacy of your own vision. And please, don't ask me to read your manuscript.

Readers Who Demand the Best

Barry Turner

All praise to J.K. Rowling for hitting the jackpot. To assume a large measure of luck in her achievement is not to deny her talent as a storyteller. As she would doubtless agree, lottery and literature are partners in advancing authors to the front of the rich list. And let that be a warning to us all. Too many aspiring writers of children's fiction have followed the footsteps of Harry Potter hoping, nearly always in vain, that some of Rowling's good fortune would rub off on to their endeavours.

Anecdotal evidence indicates that most of these offerings do not get beyond the editor's desk let alone into print. This is a measure of how good Rowling is but it also suggests that publishers may be nervous of overkill. There has been so much Harry Potter, in the books, on film and video, that it is hard to imagine any other young wizard getting a look in. True, the fantasy bandwagon has pulled *Lord of the Rings* along in its train but the Tolkien oeuvre already had a cult following. The wonder here is that it has taken so long for the movies to be made.

What will be interesting is to see if Harry Potter has real staying power. Traditionally, childhood heroes and heroines have taken their time settling in to a niche in the popular imagination. With Harry Potter it may be too much, too soon. There is a risk that he may burn out in his own special effects. Come back in ten years for the answer.

One deduction from the Harry Potter phenomenon that everyone can agree on is that the market responds well to books that appeal to young and adult readers alike. There are two sides to this argument. Many if not most books for children are bought and, to some extent, selected by their elders. Naturally, they gravitate towards books that are thought to be 'suitable', often those that they imagine would have appealed to them when they were young. Then again, as Philip Pullman has shown most recently, writing that is aimed primarily at children, if good enough, can leap the age gap to appeal to an older readership. There is nothing new in this. *Gulliver's Travels* succeeded as a tale of adventure as much as a sophisticated political satire. *Tom Brown's Schooldays* was simultaneously a reminder to fathers of what could have been and to their sons of what could be. Later school stories, such as the now unfairly forgotten *The Fifth Form at St Dominic's* by Talbot Baines Reed, depicted a scholastic ideal with equal appeal to men and boys. Dozens more books that nowadays rank as classics started their rise to literary greatness with a mighty push from their younger readers. Think only of work as varied as that of Lewis Carroll, C.S. Lewis and Roald Dahl.

But getting it right is none too easy. The starting point has to be a storyline that has youth appeal. Otherwise, however many copies are bought by adults to be handed down to the young ones, the book will ultimately fail in its prime market. The problem here is that teenagers today are far more independent, and in many crucial ways more mature than their predecessors. Looking beyond Harry Potter, what they want to read may not accord with their parents' concept of suitability. For anyone new to the twelve-plus reading habits, it can be quite an eye-opener to discover the work, say, of Melvin Burgess whose recent offering *Lady: My Life as a Bitch* is about a girl who turns herself into a dog to indulge her animal instincts. His latest book, *Doing It*, describes the fortunes of a group of teenagers in pursuit of sex. You can look in vain for the uplifting message that used to be the essential feature of any book aimed at the formative years but what you do get is first-class writing about ever-interesting topics.

If this disturbs some parents and critics, they can take comfort from the knowledge that their fears about exposing tender minds to the temptations of the flesh are echoes from the last century and earlier, although at this time the worries were more about encouraging children to gratify their primeval instincts for cruelty and violence. The brothers Grimm, who certainly lived up to their name, set the tone for a whole library of horror stories that, in their day, repelled parents as much as they delighted their intended readers. Most culpable, in adult eyes, were those writers who made a joke of barbaric behaviour, though Victorian parents were not sure what to make of Hilaire Belloc whose comic and often cruel verses about such little horrors as Matilda, who burned to death, purported to deliver a serious moral. In Matilda's case, this was the terrible punishment awaiting those who did not tell the truth. In the event, Belloc was sending up the pretensions of adults who had forgotten what it was like to be young, a joke that children understand only too well. In passing, if Belloc is still so much quoted, though nowadays chiefly by adults, why is that other great comic rhymester, Harry Graham, author of *Ruthless Rhymes*, all but ignored?

> When Grandmama fell off the boat,
> And couldn't swim (and wouldn't float),
> Matilda just stood by and smiled.
> I almost could have slapped the child.

The last edition of *Ruthless Rhymes* appeared in 1986. Note to my publisher: time for reprint?

For aspiring writers of children's fiction, the safe rule (assuming they want to earn a living) is not to try too hard to avoid offending adult sensibilities. Currently, this means dodging the brickbats from the po-faced army of political correctness. The threat to imaginative creativity is greatest in the USA where, for example, the wonderfully outrageous Roald Dahl characters have been modified to meet the requirements of the moralising minority. So it is that the gluttonous Augustus Gloop, whose 'great flabby folds of fat bulged out from every part of his body' and whose face 'was a monstrous ball of dough with two small greedy currant eyes peering out upon the world' has had to lose much of his bulk, and his perverse fascination, to avoid offending the weight disadvantaged.

The fact is that Dahl remains a children's favourite precisely because his characters cause a shock to the adult system. He is part of a noble tradition. Barrie, Carroll and Lear appealed to the subversive instincts of their young readers. Beatrix Potter and Kenneth Grahame mocked adult values (though many parents failed to notice because the provocative words were spoken by animals). The politically correct, with their scrupulous attempts not to say anything out of the way, can never reach out to reluctant readers who respond only when they are jolted by the unexpected. When Paul Jennings had to cope with a book-shy son, he fought back with a succession of macabre and risqué stories with titles such as *Uncanny! Unbelievable! and Unreal!* Jennings was soon to make impressive inroads into a whole generation of reluctant readers. They liked his punchy, no-nonsense style.

There is always a market for irreverence and fun. For juniors, two examples are *Walter and the Farting Dog* (William Kotzwinkle and Glen Murray) from Frog and *Alexander and the Terrible, Horrible, No Good, Very Bad Day* (Judith Viorst and Ray Cruz) from Aladdin. The comic naughty style of the Ahlbergs, Allan and Janet, has produced long-stayers such as *Mrs Wobble the Waitress* and *Mr Biff the*

Boxer (Puffin). For children who are a little more mature there are the *Horrible Histories* ('history with the nasty bits left in') which do get across some interesting points under the guise of parody (Scholastic).

It is the unfamiliar that sells, as proved by Scholastic, which publishes a Point Horror title every month, and by Puffin which has attracted a new audience with its all-male Fighting Fantasy characters.

A prime example of adults getting it wrong was the slavish devotion to 'relevance' in progressive education. The black spot was put on stories that harped on middle-class values, of which most youngsters had no direct experience, and on adventure that promoted outmoded assumptions of national, racial or sexual superiority. Badges of approval were awarded to recognisable characters facing up to everyday challenges in realistic circumstances. The progressives were then left to wonder why it was that young readers did not respond, indeed showed every sign of being bored out of their minds.

The explanation is to be found in a standard thesis of child psychology. It is at least thirty years ago that a Harvard academic, Jerome S. Bruner, tested his theory of the teaching of civics with two contrasting syllabuses – one based on life as we know it to be, the other on an anthropological survey of a tribe of Eskimos. The Eskimos won hands down. Bruner concluded that children learn more when their imagination is stretched beyond their immediate experience. They enjoy more too when stories venture beyond the familiar. That is why Enid Blyton reigned for so long over generations of children whose families could never have aspired to the cosy gentility of the Famous Five.

How to get started

Kate Wilson of Macmillan Children's Books and Venetia Gosling of Simon and Schuster talk to Samantha Wyndham

The newcomer to writing for children who is persuaded thus far will want to get on with the job. But where to start? This is what Kate Wilson, the head of children's publishing at Macmillan has to say. The questions are put by Samantha Wyndham.

SW: What advice would you give to newcomers to the world of writing for children?

KW: Read children's books! It is clear from many of the submissions that we receive that people do not read. They have not examined the mechanics of, say, a picture book: the proportion of text to art, the number of pages in a picture book – those fundamental things. Too many hopefuls base their writing of children's books on hazy memories of what it was like to be a child reader themselves. They are not looking at what's out there at the moment. They should be looking at the children's bestseller lists, they should be going into bookshops and looking at the books that are promoted there. That's not to say that new and original ideas, which don't in any way reflect a kind of 'me too' culture, will not emerge from nowhere and astonish us all. That sometimes happens. But even if you're going to come up with something astonishing and original and wonderful that is not like anything else on the shelves, you need to know what else is out there for you to define yourself, as it were. You need to know what there is, and why your book is different.

sw: Should the reading cover authors who were popular with earlier generations?

kw: Clearly we can all learn something from the classics. There are aspects of storytelling that are timeless. But we are talking about a rapidly changing market. Too often I see submissions that are informed by a sense of what was appropriate for children twenty or thirty years ago.

sw: What they liked when they were a child.

kw: Exactly. And things have moved on radically. Just as the toys that children play with now are very different from the toys that I played with when I was a child thirty years ago, similarly the books that children want to read are very different. We should not underestimate the shift in terms of just how quickly children grow up, including the point at which they become consumers. Today, there is so much more vying for their attention with the proliferation of TV channels and the easy access to video and DVD, not to mention the most obvious, which is the time that children spend from a very young age on computers. You have to see books in the context of all the other attractions competing for children's time.

sw: And that puts books at a disadvantage?

kw: Not necessarily. I would not be in publishing if I did not believe that books have a unique and vastly important part to play in the development of children. I think they offer things that no other medium quite achieves. Books are special in the way they make our imagination work. However, I also think it would be naïve of me, as a publisher, not to be thinking about the general cultural and media context in which books have to compete for attention.

sw: Do children's books slot into specific age ranges?

kw: You might notice that few books have definite indicators of the age at which they are aimed. This is because books can serve different purposes: a book that children may have had read to them when they were two years old can become the first book that they read for themselves when they are five years old at school. So it is difficult to be prescriptive about ages. If anything, it gets more complicated as children develop into independent readers because, of course, one 7-year-old's reading material is another 10-year-old's reading material.

sw: And girls and boys . . .?

kw: Girls and boys also *tend* to diverge. Broadly speaking I would say that there is a 0–3 range, which is predominantly board books. For the 4–5s, extending a bit to include six-year-olds, there are the standard picture books, with thirty-two pages of short stories, with lots of illustrations. Then you have a 5–7-year-olds' novel, typically with black-and-white illustrations, though a few have colour illustrations. They have a higher proportion of text. Then you have novels for the 8–12s. This is much the largest section of the market and most of the children's books that spring to people's minds fall into this category. Harry Potter is the most obvious example of a classic 8–12 fiction title. The category covers a wide range of genres, from old-fashioned magical fantasy novels and Enid Blyton adventure-style novels through to gritty contemporary issues stuff, like the books by Jacqueline Wilson. Then there is writing for teenagers, the 12-plus group. There you have writers like Melvin Burgess and

David Almond, whose novels reflect, in some way, the lives of teenagers and their preoccupations. One of the best indicators for somebody wanting to write, and thinking about age groups, would be to go to a bookshop and see how books are grouped together on the shelves. You will generally find a babies and toddlers' section, which is 0–3; a picture book section; a 5–7 fiction section; an 8–12 fiction section; and a 12-plus section. But I'm just talking about fiction here. Non-fiction is generally categorised by subject matter, not by age.

sw: Apart from having a clear idea of the target readership, what is it in a manuscript or a synopsis that makes you think it's going to make a popular book? As a specific example, what particularly attracted you to Elizabeth Laird's *A Little Piece of Ground*?[1]

kw: Elizabeth is beloved of librarians and schoolteachers, who in this context are the gatekeepers to her main audience. She has a great ability to get under the skin of people, often from radically different cultures or with radically different experiences from those that are common to her readers, at least in the UK. This is certainly true of *A Little Piece of Ground*. Moreover, the book is clearly written with absolutely overwhelming passion. To call what Elizabeth did 'research' is a huge underestimation. She lived that life, as far as she could, before she came to write that novel. But it is not a book with mass appeal. By way of a contrast, look at *The Princess Diaries* by Meg Cabot, which has a different set of qualities and a more prominent sales profile.

sw: Can you judge a manuscript by the quality of dialogue?

---

1. Based on the author's experiences in Palestine in 2002, the book describes the life of a child, Karim, who lives under the conditions of occupation.

kw: Occasionally I look at a manuscript and think, this dialogue is wonderful. But if everything else is right, I can't imagine putting a big cross against something simply on the basis that the dialogue is not the best. What is vital is that the 'voice' reflects what you are trying to put across. If you are writing a historical novel, you need to communicate a sense of the period through the voices of your characters. The hero of any Oliver Twist-style romp through nineteenth-century London like *Jammy Dodgers On The Run* needs a different kind of voice from that of a child in the twenty-first century. But it's hard to give strict guidelines. How authors handle 'dialogue' is very much part of their overall writing ability. A lot of fiction is told in a first-person narrative, a kind of internal language with which they communicate to the reader. Their 'dialogue', if you like, is with you, the reader, rather than with other characters in the book. Then the book really does have a 'voice'. Recently, one of the reasons I gave for rejecting a manuscript was that I just didn't like the 'voice'. For this book to work, you'd have to love the 'voice', you'd have to find it convincing, you'd have to want to know and like that person, and it didn't work for me.

sw: But it might work for another publisher?

kw: Of course. We are in this marvellously powerful position, as publishers, of being able to choose what is published and what is not published. But we stand or fall on the verdict of the customers. We have no pretence to making anything other than a complicated set of subjective judgements which are informed by experience and knowledge but also by personal preference.

sw: There is a view that children's writing is veering away from the cosy into a much darker realm.

kw: That is more a reflection of newspaper scare stories. In fact the sex and drugs stuff is really a tiny fraction of what is written. It is true to say that novels which try to describe contemporary everyday life for children reflect a grittier, less 'Is there honey still for tea?' kind of mood. And there are more references in teenage novels to sexual activity. But this has been happening for some time. *Forever* by Judy Blume, published over twenty-five years ago, has a graphic description of sexual intimacy between two teenagers. We can't go on regarding these things as ground-breaking. In any case, the most successful series of children's books that we have at the moment is Harry Potter. And Harry Potter is as traditional a melding of wonderful Blytonesque magic, adventure and boarding-school stuff as you could hope to find. It is, in many ways, a synthesis of all that is best of a vast, century-and-a-bit-long tradition of children's writing.

sw: Who are the principal buyers of children's books?

kw: Parents.

sw: And they then read the books themselves?

kw: Not necessarily. I have no evidence at all of the degree to which parents do or do not read children's books, with their children, to their children, or off their own bat. Research indicates that more adults are reading children's books for their own pleasure, but as to vetting or sharing the reading experience, I don't know that we have any evidence to suggest that that's happening. Then again, to say that a parent is likely just to hand over the money risks ignoring a very complicated set of interactions which might happen before the purchase. A child may say, 'Oh, I do love Jacqueline Wilson,' because a friend has bought a Jacqueline Wilson book. As members of book clubs or at school book fairs, children make their own selections but it is the parents who pay. Teachers and librarians can also influence choice.

sw: When you are looking to sign up a new author, do you consider television spin-offs, films or merchandising?

kw: Because a lot of children's books come to us via agents, we wouldn't necessarily have the screen rights as part of our portfolio. I often see books that have cinematic qualities and I am not then surprised to learn that simultaneously or subsequently, or sometimes even before, an agent has sold the film rights. Increasingly, agents use the movie potential as a way of upping the publishing anti. But one has to be careful about this because when a publisher contracts to publish a book, it is almost always published, but when film rights are bought they are bought on an option basis, and the fact that an option has been sold on a book does not in *any* way mean that there will be a Hollywood blockbuster at the end of it.

sw: Say you want to publish an illustrated book, would you prefer writer and illustrator to come as a team?

kw: There are those with an extraordinary combination of talents who can both write and illustrate, people like John Burningham, Quentin Blake, Tony Ross, Jill Murphy and Lucy Cousins. They are like hen's teeth, and are prized beyond rubies. But many good writers can't illustrate for toffee. And many good illustrators can't write for toffee. In those cases, it is up to the publisher to make a match.

sw: If you had to give one piece of advice to a newcomer, what would it be?

kw: Don't give up the day job. Very, very few authors of children's books make enough money to live on. Don't get hooked by the Harry Potter success story. Take Harry Potter out of the equation and you will find that the market is flat. And there are already a lot of books out there competing for attention.

sw: Presumably it helps if a book has international appeal.

kw: Absolutely. It is always helpful if a book isn't too nationally specific. But this is not necessarily the same thing as adopting a kind of bland international setting. It just means, for example, that if I saw a picture book manuscript which had a hedgehog crossing the road and a milk-float driving on the left-hand side of the road, swerving to avoid it, crashing into a red pillar box, and a little boy running into the red phone box and dialling 999 in order to get the police, I would take that to be a dead dog of a picture book. The hedgehog does not exist in the wild in North America, you drive on the left-hand side of the road in very few countries. Milk doesn't get delivered except in the UK, pillar boxes aren't red except in the UK, phone boxes don't look like ours anywhere else and you don't dial 999 to get the police anywhere else except in the UK. Books that are so dependent on UK settings will struggle. That's true also for books in rhyme, though there are exceptions. An obvious example is *The Gruffalo* by Julia Donaldson, a very successful picture book illustrated by Axel Scheffler, which is published in twenty-three languages, despite the fact that it is a poem. But generally, poetry or rhyme does not translate easily enough to make selling it internationally easy.

sw: If an author has something that is publishable, what is the best way of getting it looked at? Should one go to an agent rather than a publisher?

kw: Everyone thinks that they can write a children's book. Even more people think that they can write a children's book than think that they can write an adult book. The number of manuscripts that we receive with lovely, charming, thoughtful letters saying, 'I have been reading this to my granddaughter's class in school, and they all think it is absolutely fantastic, please publish it now' . . . well, if I had a pound for every one of those, then, believe me, we wouldn't be publishing books. We could make our budget in other ways.

The best advice is to start with any connections you might have with the book trade. Ask around, see if you can find somebody who knows an agent, knows a publisher, knows a bookshop person; try and find routes into the guts of the business, because getting it seen is important. The objective of an agent is to find you a publisher. The objective of a publisher is to publish a book. A publisher will not spend a vast amount of time looking at unsolicited material, and you need to be aware of that. Publishers would almost always prefer to buy direct from an author or illustrator, but they recognise that they don't necessarily have the time to find the new author or illustrator themselves. Of course, every publisher's dream is to find the gem that comes direct to them. But realistically, we buy much, much more from agents than from people sending in unsolicited manuscripts.

sw: Simply because your time needs to be dedicated to producing the books?

kw: What we should be doing is making sure that those authors and illustrators to whom we have already made a commitment are published as well as we can possibly manage. We do not have much time to read manuscripts, and people need to be aware of that. The idea that a publisher or an editorial director will be waiting for the next brown envelope to hit their desks is sadly not how we live our lives.

For a second opinion Samantha Wyndham spoke to Venetia Gosling, fiction editorial director for Simon & Schuster, who is building
a list for the nine to twelve and the seven to ten-year old age groups.
Wary of fantasy titles, an area of the market that looks to be over-
supplied, Venetia wants fresh voices, authors who can write engag-
ingly and in a contemporary style.

> 'A book for children must have a character or characters that appeal;
> the reader must want to know what is going to happen to these
> characters. The book must also have an emotional or visual appeal
> that prompts the reader to respond. Pacey dialogue is important, also
> a plot that hangs together, with good twists and turns. The story
> must be told from a child's perspective even if it takes the form of
> adult characters experiencing flashbacks to their own childhood.'

Venetia favours characters that can be extended over several
books, so giving her the opportunity to build an author as a brand.
Publishers are always on the lookout for a creative asset that they
can develop. For this reason, the second book is often more of a
challenge for new authors than the first. It is also essential to write
dialogue that children can relate to.

> 'It is important to mix with children. If you don't have your own,
> find some you can spend time with. Take note of how they speak, the
> grammar and vocabulary they use. Research your market and clearly
> define your readership; read current books already published for the
> age group or gender that you are writing for; familiarise yourself
> with publishers' current lists by looking at their catalogues or study-
> ing what is on the shelves in bookshops.'

Word lengths should be noted. Generally speaking, 8000–12,000
words is the limit for children under eight while for the eight to
twelve age group, 25,000 words is about the limit. But there are
exceptions. Simon & Schuster has a 35,000-word fiction title for ten-

year-olds on its list and a 140,000-word novel for teenagers. There is a trend in children's writing towards longer novels.

Newcomers are urged to discount the praise of pupils or children in the family. They may love your stories but that doesn't make them publishable. It is likely that children close to you are responding to the person rather than to the story itself.

Among other tips for first-time writers, Venetia recommends submissions to magazines aimed at young people.

'There are children's authors who started out as agony aunts in teen magazines. Short stories are often read by publishers on the lookout for new writers.'

But above all:

'Don't be disheartened! Even though many publishers do not accept unsolicited material [Simon & Schuster among them, professing instead to deal with agents], they *are* still looking for and launching new authors all the time – and often doing it at the expense of the already established writers with middle sale figures. Children's publishing is very front-list driven at the moment, and there is excitement about new authors.'

So You Think You Need an Agent?

Barry Turner

It used to be that the publisher invariably came first. The agent was pulled in only when the author had scored a hit or had established a track record that called for bigger and more frequent royalty cheques. But in recent years the agent has assumed more of the function of a talent spotter, ready to take on and promote newcomers who show promise. Some publishers like it this way because someone else does the hard work. Talent-spotting is a labour-intensive task and is never easy, particularly in the current climate when the market is subject to abrupt changes of fashion. Other publishers remain fiercely independent, ready to back their own judgement against the opinion of any outsider. For the first-time author, the balance has to be in favour of getting an agent at the earliest possible moment, who can shop around for the best possible deal (something few authors are capable of doing) with a publisher who is best placed to advance the writer's career. Because it is a career we are talking about. Nobody is much interested in the one-book author, particularly in fiction. To make it all worthwhile, the heavy costs of marketing a newcomer have to be spread over several titles.

The contract

A good agent is interested in money, but not exclusively so. He, or, increasingly nowadays, she, will negotiate a contract that illuminates the small print. This is more important than it sounds. The simple agreement to publish, a two- or three-page document much favoured by publishers of the old school, has typically grown to fifteen pages or more. This is in order to encompass book club deals, promotion budgets, cover design, the timing of publication, print number and subsidiary rights – the latter capable of attracting earnings long after the book is out of print. The sheer range of potential subsidiary rights is mind-boggling – overseas publication (the publisher will try for world rights but when an agent is acting, US and translation rights are nearly always held back), film and television adaptations, audio cassettes, video, to mention only the most obvious. A book does not have to be a bestseller to earn advances and royalties in several countries, languages and formats. These are sums which in themselves may be quite small but which can add up to a healthy income. A writer acting on his own behalf is unlikely to realise all the possibilities.

Approaching an agent

But back to basics. If an agent is required, where best to find one? Go through the list on page 148 to see who handles the sort of work that interests you. But be warned, there is no sure way of matching a writer and agent merely by glancing over names and addresses. The famous names exercise the heaviest clout, of course, but the most powerful agencies are not necessarily suitable for a beginner who may feel the need for the close personal contact offered by a smaller agency. On the other hand, the smaller agency may already have taken on its full quota of newcomers. Those who are struggling for a toehold in publishing are by definition low earners who must, for a time, be subsidised by the more profitable sector of a client list. The agent who gets the balance wrong is heading for the bankruptcy court.

Advice frequently given by the happily agented to the agentless is to seek out the opinion of authors who have been through the mill and to learn from their experiences. Writers' circles and seminars organised by the Society of Authors are fruitful sources of gossip.

Once the prime choice is identified, there remains the formidable problem of persuading the agent that you are next in line for stardom. Start with the knowledge that unsolicited manuscripts clog the agent's post. An average intake is thirty to fifty packages a month but two agents are in the eighty to one hundred category and one agent receives more than 150. Of these submissions, less than five per cent show real promise. An agent who receives twenty to thirty unsolicited manuscripts a month reports 'five strong leads in fourteen years'.

Of course, they are keen to bag the next Philip Pullman or J.K. Rowling but experience tells them that the odds are against finding them in the morning's post. They need to be persuaded that your offering is something special. To achieve this, it is essential to put some effort into presentation. What follows applies to approaching publishers just as much as to approaching agents. If you do decide to make a direct approach to a publisher, and there may be very good reasons for doing so such as knowing someone who works on the children's list or, having failed to come up with an agent you can work with, choosing to conduct your own business, the challenge is still to make your pitch as strong as possible. A grimy manuscript, frayed at the edges, typed single spaced with loads of corrections, tied up in a bundle which comes apart on delivery, will not – surprise, surprise – get a fulsome welcome. Obvious? Maybe, but it happens all the time.

To seek a professional opinion, you too must be professional. In writing to an agent or publisher set out your wares in the most attractive way possible. Start with a few lines of justification. What is the book about? Why does it cry out to be written? This is where you recall the central idea that started you on your way. Having settled on a snappy justification, the synopsis can be used to describe the book in some detail. It is impossible to specify length but two or three pages should do it. What is essential is for the synopsis to be a clear and logical description of the book. It should be typewritten or word processed with double spacing.

Along with all this go some sample chapters. Even if you have a finished manuscript, it is unwise at this stage to send off the whole thing. A sample is easier to digest and if it is tasty enough, the agent or publisher will soon come back for more. The covering letter of introduction should say who you are, what you do and whether you have been published before in whatever form. Never email. Have you seen what a manuscript can do to gum up the technological works?

More advice on related matters comes from a *Writer's Handbook* survey of agents, most of which applies every bit as firmly when corresponding with publishers.

- Write – don't telephone – to one agent at a time, sending a brief covering letter to the agent concerned. Too often authors send photocopies addressed 'Dear Sir/Madam' so it is obvious all the agents in this book are being approached at the same time. These go straight into the bin.
- Do not submit to publishers first and then decide to use an agent without admitting that publishers have already rejected

your proposals. Either write direct to publishers or use an agent from the outset.

- Always enclose return postage – preferably a stamped envelope – and a stamped card if you want an acknowledgement.
- *Always* keep a copy of any material submitted – don't use registered post or recorded delivery as this can entail collection from a distant post office – and allow at least a month for a response.

Do not be disappointed if an agent, or even several agents give the thumbs down. They may be overloaded with clients. But even if this is not so, remember that all writing is in the realm of value judgement. Where one agent fails to see talent, another may be more perceptive. The only advice is to keep trying.

In the event of a rejection, do not expect as of right a detailed analysis of where you may be going wrong. Agents and publishers tend to get upset when they are asked to give free advice. Life is complicated enough as it is.

Commission, royalties and fees

Agents do not come free. Asking for 10 per cent of your earnings is standard but an increasing number go for 15 per cent and a few pitch as high as 17.5 or 20 per cent – plus VAT. A VAT-able author can reclaim the tax. Others must add 17.5 per cent of the commission to calculate the agent's deduction from earnings. Some agents invoice certain administrative costs such as photocopying but no reputable agent charges a reading fee. There are too many scandals attached to reading fees, one of the easiest ways for the unscrupulous to make money from the gullible. It is sometimes argued that if an agent is paid to assess the value of a manuscript, he's bound to give it full attention. Maybe. But if there are responsible agents who justify a reading fee, they are most certainly outnumbered by the charlatans who take the money and run.

When the day comes (perhaps this should read, *if* the day comes, but we are taking a positive line) that an agent or publisher shows an interest in your manuscript, discussion must inevitably turn to the financial deal that will secure the best possible return on your labour and talent. If an agent is acting as the front man, he will eventually come back with an offer contained within a publisher's contract which may or may not be acceptable. That's up to you and your bank manager. If you are dealing direct with a publisher and have no experience of contracts, the Minimum Terms Agreement (MTA), formulated by the Society of Authors and the Writers' Guild and accepted by most of the leading publishers, is a useful bench-mark. A copy can be obtained from either the Society of Authors or the Writers' Guild (free of charge to members who send a stamped, addressed envelope). One of the great virtues of the MTA is that it guarantees an author's involvement in every stage of publication, from jacket design through to catalogue copy.

Where the MTA is less assertive is on the question of royalties. Old hands remember the days where it was standard for a publisher to offer 10 per cent on hardback and 7.5 per cent on paperback with built-in increases tied to volume of sales. No longer. High-pressure marketing now requires a more flexible approach. Concessions to powerful booksellers by way of increased discounts have to be paid for and it can well be that the writer is asked to take a lower royalty so that his book may be sold more aggressively. Fair or unfair? Who is to say until the cheque arrives in the post and the author jumps for joy or rings the Samaritans.

Any author who wants to make a living by writing must establish early on that his publisher is prepared to make an advance payment on account of royalties. The bigger the advance the more likely the publisher will be to put his back into the marketing effort. Even if he winds up hating the book, he will want to earn his money back by pushing sales.

But be warned that advances for children's books are among the lowest in the industry, chiefly because the books are shorter and the cover prices correspondingly cheaper. The highly publicised mega deals are not typical. Over most of children's publishing, an advance of £1000 to £2000 is not unusual. The advance should be non-returnable, except when the author fails to deliver a manuscript by the due date, or if it is not in line with what was agreed with the publisher. Usually, it is split three ways, part on signature of contract, part on delivery of the manuscript and part on publication. What proportion of the advance will be due on signature? Ideally one-third (or more if you can present a good case) with the remaining two-thirds due on delivery and publication respectively.

Before you sign

As a spot check on the acceptability of a contract, confirm four essential points before you sign.

First, there should be an unconditional commitment to publish the book within a specified time, say, twelve months from delivery of the typescript, or, if the typescript is already with the publisher, from signature of the agreement.

The obligation to publish should not be subject to approval or acceptance of the manuscript. Otherwise what looks like a firm contract may be little more than an unenforceable declaration of intent to publish. It is equally important to watch that the words 'approval' or 'acceptance' do not appear in the clause relating to the advance payment. This point about the publisher's commitment to publishing a book is of vital importance, particularly since publishers' editors change jobs with increasing frequency. An author who has started a book with enthusiastic support from his editor may, when he delivers it, find he is in the hands of someone with quite different tastes and ideas who then asks for changes.

Secondly, there should be a proper termination clause. This should operate when the publishers fail to comply with any of the provisions of the contract or if, after all editions of the work are out of print or off the market, they have not, within six months of a written request, issued a new edition or impression of at least 1,500 copies.

Thirdly, there should not be an option clause that imposes unreasonable restrictions on future works. The best advice is to strike out the option clause but if this proves impossible, an option should be limited to one book on terms to be mutually agreed (not 'on the same terms').

Finally, get it in writing. A recent article in *The Author* says it all: 'Your editor may be wonderful. Your faith in human nature may be undented. It may seem pedantic, pushy, bossy. But if you ever agree something important with a publisher which is not in your contract – be it regarding deadlines, amendments, publicity or, especially, money – follow up the meeting or conversation with a friendly letter, confirming the salient points. If things go wrong and all you have is the memory of an airy promise on the telephone that the publisher has since "forgotten", you will be in a much stronger position if you can produce a copy of a letter as evidence of that promise.'

Marketing

Success begets success. An author who makes a hit can usually rely on his publisher's marketing team to help him repeat the trick. While it is only the super-earners who qualify for an advertising campaign, there will be bookshop promotions with eye-catching displays conveniently close to the till. Then there are the literary editors to be solicited for reviews and the feature pages to fill with author interviews. In the week of publication the author may be taken off round the country to talk about his 'number one bestseller' on radio and television. Outrageous hype is part of the game and has been with us for a long time. Go with it. It may not be your idea of fun but it is all part of a carefully orchestrated campaign to put your name before the public and to have them equate it with books that must be bought.

No writer can ask for more.

Letting the Facts Speak

John Malam, an established non-fiction author,
on earning a living by writing to order

Children's non-fiction covers a host of virtues and as many, if not more, sins. It is a category defined by what it is not – it is *not* fiction – rather than by what it is. While some non-fiction books are solid information or fact books (ones that children are encouraged to use at school), others adopt a story-like style and become narrative non-fiction, replete with invented characters, dialogue and imaginary settings, through which runs a stream of truth. The same book may be shelved in the 'information' section of a library, yet a bookshop may categorise it as 'reference'. So it is, that 'non-fiction' is an umbrella term for a wide range of books.

For writers who venture into the world of children's non-fiction, where the objective is to impart information in a clear and concise style, there can be a steady supply of work from a range of clients and, as finished books enter the UK public library system, there's the prospect of an annual payment from the Public Lending Right scheme – the nearest thing to a royalty many non-fiction authors will receive.

Bookshops, libraries and schools

Just as children's fiction can be sub-divided into categories (books for beginner readers, ones for confident readers, teen fiction, and so on), non-fiction is also targeted at specific markets. The major division is between books published for sale through high street retailers, and those that will spend their working lives as library books. While the former are titles with wide popular appeal – anything from an ephemeral title about, say, text messaging, to a heavyweight encyclopaedia – the latter tend to be subject-specific tools: resources created in response to the needs of schools. Non-fiction books are invariably age-specific, frequently linked to the bands of the National Curriculum.

The ideas factory

A key difference between fiction and non-fiction is where the initial idea for a new book comes from. While fiction generally stems from an original idea plucked from who-knows-where by an author, non-fiction has a more methodical genesis. Typically, a publisher or packager (an independent product developer) conceives the title in-house. Rarely do freelance authors submit successful ideas of their own but, if they do, the odds are on finding that, by some strange coincidence, a publisher has already come up with an almost identical proposal. Should this ever happen to you, interpret it as a sign that there are very few completely original ideas when it comes to writing children's non-fiction – facts are facts: it's what you do with them that counts.

Bear in mind that publishers and packagers should know the market better than anyone. They know what to supply it with, they know what they can produce, they know what they can sell – not now, but at some point within the next twelve months or so, which is how far ahead they usually look. What they need are people to make their idea a reality – someone to write the words (author), someone to draw the pictures (illustrator), someone to locate the images (picture researcher), someone to join the pieces together (designer), someone to check the author's facts (expert consultant), and someone to co-ordinate this scattered group from start to finish, issue instructions, dot the i's and cross the t's, while all the time keeping an eye on the clock and the budget (editor). The author is part of this time-honoured team of freelance and in-house profes- sionals, each with an essential contribution to make. There's no room for a prima donna or a jobsworth.

Writer for hire

Aspiring authors must make it their business to circulate their CVs (both paper and electronic) to let editors know who they are, what they've written (or what they can write about), and what, if any- thing, they specialise in. If the writer's experience fits the editor's requirements, a match is made and a project gets started. While some projects might only require generalist writers, able to turn their skills to a range of topics, others may call for specialists with in-depth subject knowledge and authority. It's the editor's decision but, equally, an author should feel confident that they are the right person for the job. It's easier to turn down a project than to start one, then withdraw from it at a late stage in its development.

Chances are, the publisher or packager will have already pro- duced sample material to whet appetites for the book. This is usually the book cover and some pages from it, mocked-up with dummy text and pictures to look like the real thing. Its sole purpose is to be shown to potential customers (buyers in bookshop chains, schools and libraries, and overseas distributors). It's designed to gauge whether there's life in a project, or not. If the reaction is positive and orders are forthcoming, that's when the editor has real need of an author.

The editor briefs the author about the project, outlining details such as book title, number of pages, page size (width and height), intended age-range, estimated number of words per spread, whether there are to be side-bars and panels with text separate from the main material, what sort of images will be used (illustrations, photographs, or both), if there's to be a resource section (glossary, further information, index), and what the deadline and payment terms are. Importantly, the editor will outline the writing style the author should follow. This can be virtually anything, from the didactic to the humorous. If mock-up material has been produced, the editor sends copies to the author – it's a visual interpretation of the brief, showing exactly what the publisher or packager is setting out to create. Authors generally find mock-ups useful, as they can see exactly how the book is expected to shape up.

However, a brief can be a movable feast, with changes sprung on the author who has little choice but to go along with them (the number of pages are reduced; the word count is increased). Remember, we're describing a commissioned book, where the author is under contract to work to a plan.

Research is the key skill

As US screenwriter Wilson Mizner put it: 'Copy from one, it's plagiarism; copy from two, it's research.' This is good advice for any non-fiction author. Research is at the heart of all non-fiction writing. To do the job, and to do it well, an author has to be persistent in the search for information, consistent in the use of facts, and accurate in how knowledge is used and interpreted. Equally, a children's non-fiction author should be aware of what will excite and inform a young reader, and what will not. Knowing where to find information and, importantly, checking that it is reliable, are essential research skills that any self-respecting non-fiction author must have. A specialist author should be aware of the latest developments in the field, so current knowledge can be filtered and passed on to children, giving the book a competitive advantage over one written by a non-specialist.

While some books are relatively easy to research, using libraries, museums and reputable websites, others require a more journalistic approach, interviewing contacts and visiting relevant places. However the research is done, the underlying function is essentially the same – a quest for knowledge that an author can put into a learning context for children, enabling them to grasp a concept, follow a sequence, perform an instruction, and so on. For most authors, the research phase is the hardest part of the job. It's when they invest the most time, gathering a mass of data from which they will select what will – and what will not – make it through to the final draft of the book.

The synopsis – a promise to make and keep

In common with fiction, a non-fiction book starts off with a synopsis. Briefed by the editor, the author knows the project parameters. If a book is conceived as a thirty-two page title, it's no good submitting a synopsis for one with forty-eight pages (books are typically planned with pages in multiples of 16–32, 48, 64, 80, 96, 112, 128, etc, with illustrated non-fiction information titles favouring the lower page extents).

The synopsis is the book structure in outline, designed to show both author and editor how the subject will be treated. It's when the author puts the research data into order, boiling it down to little more than a list of key points that will be covered on each double-page spread, or in each chapter. Think of it as the author's promise to the editor of things to come. But it's more than merely a bullet-point description of the narrative (where narrative includes main text, plus text that is to appear in side-bars and panels). A children's non-fiction author also has to think about the visual content of the book, and this is where the non-fiction synopsis is significantly different to that of a fiction book.

The author is responsible for giving guidance on what illustrations are to be drawn, and what photos will be needed. If the book is to have original illustrations, the synopsis should contain instructions for what is to be drawn. These can be written instructions ('on page eight we need to see a cross-section through a volcano for the main illustration, and also a series of smaller pictures showing the different types of volcano – cone, fissure, shield, composite'), or photocopies of images taken from existing books. This is not to say the illustrator has to copy the author's instructions to the letter. Rather, it's a way of easing an illustrator into a project, suggesting what the author has in mind.

Sometimes, the quickest and clearest method of communicating visual ideas is for the author to sketch things out. No one expects the author to be an artist, but anything is better than nothing at all. Another method is to take snapshots, particularly of details that are difficult to describe or unlikely for the illustrator to locate independently. For example, when I was commissioned to write a book on how a hospital works, the illustrator based his pictures on photos I took as I went behind the scenes in every department, seeing equipment and procedures the public are unaware of. Had I not done this, I would have been faced with countless requests for picture reference. Worse still, the illustrator might have misinter-preted the written instructions and drawn the wrong piece of equipment, or put people in incorrect poses for the tasks I was writing about.

If a book is to have photos, then the author should itemise what's required ('page 20 – a close-up photo of a shark's jaw; page 44 – a photo of a surfboard bitten by a shark'). This 'wants' list is used by a picture researcher, whose job is to obtain photos from commercial picture libraries, private collections, museums, and so on.

A non-fiction synopsis can end up as a lengthy document, and it's not uncommon for it to have as many (or more) words as the finished book. And when the synopsis is written, and the editor has approved it, only then is it time to start writing.

Two ways to write the book

A non-fiction book is either text-led or design-led. If it's text-led, the author will be required to submit the stated amount of words (or near enough), following the synopsis. The editor will then work closely with the designer, illustrator and picture researcher, bringing together the different elements (words, illustrations, photos) to produce page layouts. The author is sent a set of layouts to check and amend as necessary. Ideally they should be provided as paper printouts, but sometimes they arrive as electronic files on disc, or by email attachment.

If the book is design-led, the text will be the last thing to slot into place. The other team members will do their bit, working closely to the author's synopsis. The end result will still be page layouts – but with gaps left for the text. Again, the layouts come to the author who 'writes to fit'. This is both a pleasurable and an inconvenient way to write. On the one hand the author can see how much (or how little) text is needed. On the other, it can be nigh-on impossible to condense an idea so it fits the space allocated to it. All is not lost, since the layouts can usually be re-jigged to free-up space for the text.

Clarity of expression is essential. The maxim of 'one thought in one sentence' could have been devised for non-fiction writing. It's hard to put this into practice without a text degenerating into staccato prose, but for the very young, or for reluctant readers, this may be just what is required.

Whichever way the text is written, the author should ideally be involved in the layout process and be invited to comment on illustrations, photos, page design and relationship of text to the other elements. Not every publisher or packager consults the author at this stage, but it's better for everyone if they do. As the layouts gradually evolve into the finished designs of the book, the author will be asked to write captions for illustrations and photos, compile a glossary based on the final, edited version of the text and, if an indexer is not to hand, produce an index, too. After this, the book is sent to the printer's, which can be anywhere in the world. A colour proof of every page is produced, which the editor checks. Sometimes the author checks the colour proofs, too, but if not, then the next thing he sees is finished copies of the book.

Getting started in non-fiction

There is no special route that leads an aspiring author into writing children's non-fiction. Suffice to say that a liking for working with informational texts is a prerequisite to success, as is the skill to ferret out nuggets of knowledge from a plethora of sources.

Many children's non-fiction authors have worked in-house as editors, before swapping roles, as I did. As editors they will have commissioned texts for their employer's books, and will have guided them on their way to publication. They have a distinct advantage as they understand the creative process, knowing who does what, when, why and how. This is not to say there is no way in for those without editorial experience, but it would be misleading to suggest the doors are wide open. It's in editors' interests to find new talent, and if you have something to offer, it's up to you to do some basic market research. Familiarise yourself with who non-fiction publishers are, and what they are currently publishing – then contact individual editors and introduce yourself.

Those with specialist knowledge are in a strong position. A teacher with experience of special educational needs may be matched by an educational publisher to a project about dyslexia or attention deficit disorder. A biologist or geneticist writing about genes and DNA is preferred to someone who's not been near a microscope since schooldays. An historian will make a better job of a book about Mesopotamia than someone who's never heard of the place. Equally, experts may find themselves recruited as consultants or researchers, commissioned to work with an experienced author who translates their knowledge into child-friendly text.

Copyright, deadlines, agents and money

And finally, the bottom line. Children's non-fiction authors seldom retain copyright in their books. Deadlines for delivery of text can be frighteningly short. Agents rarely want to represent children's non-fiction authors. Flat fees are the norm, and royalties are usually out of the question.

Why don't authors retain copyright in their work? Let's put it like this: whose work is it? Sure, the author has written the text, but if it's a commissioned book, then the idea has probably come from a publisher or packager, so they regard ownership as theirs, lock, stock, and full stop. Contracts spell this out in excruciating detail, demanding authors sign away a whole swathe of rights that would make a fiction author or agent reach for the red pen. You sign it to get paid, and in return you give up any continuing interest in the book. Thereafter, you really don't want to know if it goes on to sell a million copies, is translated into a dozen languages, or is reissued some years later with a changed title to make it seem 'new'. No, you really don't want to know this.

Why are the deadlines tight? The usual reason is because a publisher or packager is already committed to publishing the book on a given date, and working back from that dictates how much time is available for writing, illustrating, designing, printing, shipping and distributing the book. I once accepted a commission for a TV tie-in book. The series was to be screened in January, and it went without saying that the book had to be in the shops at that time. I was contacted in October and given the brief for the book – forty-eight-pages of interviews, activities, things to make, and information about the historical period of the series. It was a tall order, made even more demanding by the fact that there was to be a press launch the second week in December for the series and the books (there was an adult book too, commissioned long before the children's book). Working back from this date gave me little more than three weeks to research it, write it and check layouts. On the very day of the launch, finished books arrived from the printer's in Belgium. I'm sure the ink was still tacky. Admittedly, this is an extreme example of a tight deadline, and corners were cut to meet it. A more realistic schedule is outlined in the panel on page 44.

Why don't agents represent children's non-fiction authors? Two reasons: money and insider knowledge. An agent will usually take a 10 per cent slice of an author's income from a book, though it can be as much as fifteen per cent. Given that non-fiction books pay flat fees, not royalties, and the financial offer can be, and often is, modest, there's not enough in it to make it worthwhile for an agent. Another reason is that non-fiction authors know as well as anyone in the business who publishes what, and which editor works where. There's no need for a go-between to drum up work for authors who are perfectly capable of finding their own. And if you think an agent might be able to improve a fee, think again. The editor is looking to hire a writer, and if Person A is too expensive, then Person B's phone will ring. This is not to say fees are non-negotiable, and an author (whether a new one or an old hand) should not be averse to asking for more, for whatever reason. Politely informing a stingy publisher or packager of the better rates offered by others will not only educate them but, hopefully, gain a better offer.

So, what are the fees? Rates vary between firms, and according to the nature of the project. While one firm may offer £1,500 for a thirty-two-page book (this is pretty much the going-rate), another will offer £1,000 or less, justifying it on the grounds that little text is needed, yet just as much effort may be needed by the author from start to finish. Payment is usually made in three stages – signature of contract, delivery of text and checking of layouts or proofs. Yes, these are low fees but libraries are buying fewer books and bookshops stock only a limited range of children's non-fiction titles. The knock-on is smaller print-runs that generate lower incomes – hence there is less in the budget for authors, illustrators, and so on.

Other commissions a writer can seek out include writing for magazines and partworks, or contributing to multi-author volumes, such as encyclopaedias. In these cases, authors are usually paid rates of between £100 and £200 per thousand words.

Established children's non-fiction authors who write for fees do so knowing that to make a living they have to be adept at keeping several projects running simultaneously. Incomes can be supplemented by making school visits, which pay well and on time, and there's always the PLR payment to look forward to each February, plus payments made by the Authors' Licensing and Collecting Society (ALCS) for works which are photocopied by schools.

Despite the obvious drawbacks of writing children's non-fiction, there's nothing more satisfying than spending a day in a school, talking to children, their parents and teachers, and seeing how a class uses non-fiction books which, to their writer, feel like 'children'. All thoughts of being on a 'writing treadmill' evaporate, until emails, answerphone messages, faxes and letters are picked up that night, bringing with them the usual range of editorial queries and, hopefully, offers of new work.

Sample schedule for a non-fiction book

September	publisher/packager has idea for new book
October	publisher/packager takes mocked-up sample material to the Frankfurt International Book Fair; starts selling the idea to build up a viable print run
November	editor contacts author with briefs about the project
February	deadline for delivery of text
March/April	publisher/packager takes text and artwork to the London International Book Fair and the Bologna Children's Book Fair (the big one in children's publishing); continues to build up a viable print run
May/June	final development of page layouts; colour proofs produced
July/August	book is printed; bulk stock shipped to warehouse; copies distributed to bookshops, schools and libraries
September	publication, at the start of a new school year

John Malam (www.johnmalam.co.uk) *is an established non-fiction author who has written more than one hundred information books for children.* He is the children's book reviewer for the Manchester Evening News, *and makes frequent visits to schools where he talks about his work as a children's author.*

Writers on Writing

Drawing on the combined experience of a leading group of children's writers, here are their responses to the questions most frequently asked by those trying to break in to the magic circle.

Getting started

'What or where is the starting point?' As Chairman of the Society of Authors, Children's Writers and Illustrators Group, Tony Bradman, who writes mostly picture books and young fiction, is used to responding to this conversation opener.

'I didn't really choose to concentrate on writing for children. I'd always wanted to be a writer (from the age of twelve!), but I'd thought I was going to write for adults. Then I became a dad and started reading children's books to my own kids; reviewing them and interviewing children's writers. Pretty soon I knew that's what I wanted to do. I wrote some stories and some rhymes for my own children, then eventually was asked by a publisher if I'd ever thought of writing for kids. I showed them some of my rhymes and they became my first book.'

For Susan Davis, writing for teenagers came about purely by chance.

'I always imagined I was writing for adults, and while my short fiction had been widely published, my novels weren't quite hitting the mark. I had written a book called *The Henry Game* which had a sixteen-year-old protagonist. This was set in the seventies and based partly on my own teenage years. When my agent saw it she told me I should set it in the present day and generally update it for the teen market. Having followed her advice, the book was quickly taken up by Random House and Transworld.'

The route via adult fiction was also taken by Louise Cooper who has published more than fifty novels and who likes to write stories to send a shiver down the spine.

'Until 1994 virtually all my books were for an adult readership. But then I was approached by a senior editor at Hodder, who had read my "Time Master" fantasy series and asked me if I would consider writing a children's trilogy set in the same imaginary world. The result was the "Daughter of Storms" trilogy, and it got me hooked on children's writing. Making a living in the adult market was also becoming difficult for me at the time, so the chance to switch my concentration to a younger readership was a practical blessing as well, and I've not looked back since.'

That it is fate more than design that propels writers towards writing for children is a recurring theme. Here is Richard Platt, creator of dozens of picture books and narrative non-fiction.

'I was writing books about photography, and as cameras became more automatic, I figured that I would soon be out of work. I was offered a job as an editor at a children's publisher, and through this connection began writing 'how-to' photography books for kids. I had a lot of knowledge about photography and I have always been able to express myself in writing. So it seemed natural to combine the two things.

I started writing *children's* books because the publishers I was working for were planning a book on the cinema, and my background in photography made me a sensible choice as author. They approached me.'

Beth Webb, whose nine published books include three about a cat called Fleabag and who has designed a university-level correspondence course on writing for children, also admits to an element of chance.

'I started by writing stories for my own four children. I was an ex-journalist and radio broadcaster, so I had some idea about using words, but I didn't really start until I did my MA in creative writing about four years ago. Also, I like a story to be simply and clearly told. I feel much adult fiction is getting too complex with the current fashions for creating whole 'world-scapes' and increasingly esoteric ways of communicating ideas. Give me a well-told story any day. It seems to be principally within so-called 'children's fiction' that this is still allowed to happen. And I'm a big kid, I write stories I want to read. Why not?'

And Jana Novotny Hunter, another who teaches writing and writes for all age groups from toddlers to teenagers, came to children's books as a prospective illustrator.

'I took a class on illustration and when I discovered we had to write the books too, I almost left! I was living in the USA so I went on to attend some excellent classes at UCLA on writing for children. I am a firm believer in learning your craft while developing your talents.'

'Where do the ideas come from? Is there a particular source of inspiration that we can all tap into?' Again, there is a wide measure of agreement. Let Beth Webb speak for all our interviewees.

'You have to be inspired by children to write effectively for them. I take a notebook everywhere I go and write down questions and comments and thoughts that children come out with. These are perfect starting points.

You *have* to be able to see the world through the eyes, ears and heart of a child of the age you are writing for. Oliver Postgate (inventor of "Noggin the Nog", "Ivor the Engine" and "Bagpuss") said in his autobiography that he once visited the home he lived in when he was a small child, but he didn't recognise it . . . until he got onto his knees and looked at it from the height of a three-year-old . . .

. . . *Then* he saw the drainpipe, the wonky gate, the window sill from below . . . it all came back into focus. You have to be prepared to get down onto the hands and knees of your memory and imagination and see the world from the perspective of your reader at the stage they are at. This is the key to beginning to communicate in a meaningful way.'

The ability to think like a child is clearly an advantage. Here is Louise Cooper.

'I find that children's imaginations and ability to think laterally without effort have helped fire me when it comes to developing new ideas. Mostly, though, I think my plots come from my own imagination. It's probably no exaggeration to say that the majority of my ideas are the result of dreams – mine have always been bizarre – or daydreams; a process that involves wandering around the house or garden with a vacant expression and a mind that's off in another world. My husband has invented a new verb for it: "vaguing". The other major source of ideas is the "what if" factor. It can be triggered by anything, however trivial: a snatch of overheard conversation, a small item in the local paper, something I notice in passing when I'm out and about. It catches my interest. I think "What if . . .?" and I start inventing a story that expands and explores that one small moment.

A couple of examples: a ruined church, glimpsed briefly over a hedge while driving through Norfolk years ago was the sole inspiration for my recent book *Hunter's Moon* (Hodder), and a rickety cupboard door with a handle that kept falling off gave rise to a recently completed synopsis.'

Successful children's writers do seem to have the talent of reliving their past. Susan Davis has 'vivid memories of my teenage years' though she has to keep up to date with fashion and language by dipping into current teen magazines such as *Mizz* and *J17*. Having children in the family can help too. When Richard Platt develops a story . . .

'I often have a particular child in mind as a model for the character. For example, Jake Carpenter, in my recent book *Pirate Diary*, was based on my wife's grandson Jacob.'

Keeping children's attention

Now it begins to get difficult. Children are among the most unforgiving critics. If the subject or story does not immediately grab attention, then the book is liable to be relegated to the junk pile. The best advice on how to avoid this humiliation comes from Catherine and Laurence Anholt, double Gold Award winners of the Smarties Book Prize, whose website (www.anholt.co.uk) is particularly helpful to aspiring writers.

'Language is everything – it is essential to find your own, personal, confident "voice". Write in an easy-going, natural style as if you are speaking confidently or telling an anecdote. Allow the ideas to come from a deep level – find the POETRY in words; enjoy their SOUNDS. Play with rhythms, alliterations and rhyme. Invent words. Dig out extraordinary, funny or unexpected words. Quentin Blake says that he needed to draw a hundred miles of line before he became confident as an artist; similarly, an author needs to write very regularly in order to build up momentum. It can be helpful to have several different ideas "on the go" in order to avoid becoming too precious.'

What about characters? The Anholts say:

'Think about traditional fairy tales, or pantomime characters, look at Roald Dahl or Dickens again – the characters are always three-dimensional; never flat – often REALLY bad or REALLY creepy or REALLY silly. Don't be afraid to "Ham It Up" a bit when writing for children. If your characters are going to be children, make them "come alive" by observing real children – young kids are like little whirlwinds – they race about and charge through a whole cascade of emotions within a day. They cry, laugh, get scared. They are funny, slightly crazy, unpredictable. They have huge ambitions and aspirations. They lead lives that are charged with emotion as friendships twist and turn. Modern families are bubbling stews of emotion, as parents try to resolve all their complicated issues of gender, divorce, step-families and so on; children soak all that up.'

When writing for older children, the first hurdle for Beth Webb is persuading a browser to take the book down from the shelf.

'Sales hype helps here, as do "grabbing" cover illustrations. Sadly that's all out of the author's hands so if possible, choose a publisher that is good at sales and marketing. But once you have a reader inside the cover of a book, you have to write a really grabbing first sentence, paragraph and page. You have to compel the reader to read on. For that, you need a touch of "magic" and a great deal of skill. The opening must also contain thoughts, emotions, situation and ideas that the reader can relate to. I work with a great many children teaching them creative writing. The stories my students come up with most of all are: fantasy, comedy, horror and real-life. So I take that on board and try to bring an element of all of these into the stories I write.

But, underneath all of these things, the story must always be about an element of reality, something that speaks about the facts of the reader's own life. The story may be pure fantasy, but it is what it is ABOUT that matters: e.g. step-parenting is a big issue in the story of King Arthur. By all means tell the tale of the boy in Merlin's care, but make sure the story is ABOUT how Arthur copes with the loss of his mother, not knowing who his father is and having an overbearing foster brother he can't stand.'

Susan Davis agrees that teenagers have a low boredom threshold, so to catch their interest the writing must grab them from the first page.

'However, writing cold-bloodedly for a particular market rarely works. Personally I loathe issue-led fiction. For me, the characters are the most important feature. They must seem like real, convincing people readers can relate to. My own books are a quirky mixture of humour, history and the supernatural, set against a contemporary background. This is the kind of thing I like to write primarily for myself. I have to think "Does this excite me?" rather than, "Will this excite my teenage audience?"'

A cautionary note on bringing in contemporary issues comes from Louise Cooper.

'It may be that some will emerge as a by-product of the story, but I never deliberately set out to tackle them. My priority – or ground rule – is to tell a gripping and entertaining tale with a strong beginning, a satisfying end, and enough in the middle to hold my readers' attention and keep them turning the pages. Children *are*

interested in contemporary issues, of course, but I feel the emphasis
on this can be overdone, to the detriment of entertainment – and
entertainment should be a novelist's first priority. We all need some
escapism in our lives, after all!'

Jana Novotny Hunter feels strongly that it is important to offer a
value system which is supportive to her teenage readers.

'With this in mind, I confine sex to passionate kisses (although I
wouldn't rule out more if that was the story I wanted to tell). I steer
away from drugs altogether, out of a personal preference. As long as
drug-taking is dealt with in a responsible way, it is appropriate for a
teenage audience, but I prefer not to be the one to do it.'

Illustrations and websites

A persistent worry for authors who are new to children's writing is
what to do about illustrations. Assuming that you are not multi-
talented, what is the best way forward? To approach an illustrator
with an offer to work in partnership? Our panel advises against
this. If the idea is strong enough, the publisher will come up with
his own thoughts on illustrations and will almost certainly have an
address list of artists who can be matched with particular projects.

The only occasion when you will be compelled to find your own
illustrator is in the event of choosing the self-publishing route. In
this case, personal contact counts for a lot though a wanted ad in
The Author, the quarterly journal of The Society of Authors, may
bring results. But be prepared to pay up front. It is unlikely that an
illustrator of any worth will be ready to share with you the risk of
disappointing sales.

How important is it to establish a website? Tony Bradman is not
sure it is worth having 'although that's probably because I haven't

got one.' He adds, 'I've been meaning to do something about it, but just haven't had the time; too busy writing.' By contrast, Beth Webb thinks it is essential to be linked up to the internet.

'Children expect it, and it's a good way to get your other titles advertised as well. If a bookshop only has one of your titles on the shelf, the readers won't know you have eight or nine others unless you tell them! Parents and teachers like it, too. They can "check up" on who you are. They can decide whether you are a suitable sort of author for them to promote. Publishers looking for writers can find you as well. There are loads of useful links you can create from your site to other sites, and if you provide links, other sites link to you as well, which is really good from a promotional point of view. As to design, there are really good companies like Wordpool who specialise in helping authors. In the end, I went to Realmdesign, and the webmaster there really looked at my work carefully and thought about the essence of my stories, then incorporated all of this in the site.'

One possible advantage of having a website is being able to push for work that relates to children's writing such as lectures, reviews and broadcasting. The downside is that many of the offers that come through have no paycheque attached. Local radio can be fun but at best it is an opportunity to promote your books. Lectures and festival appearances are usually rewarded but the fees are modest and it is as well to check out beforehand that some money is on the table.

A website link to Amazon can be a money earner, as Richard Platt reveals.

'This on-line book retailer pays a small percentage of the sale price of books to the owner of any site that directs buyers to Amazon.com. This means that if someone looks at your site and clicks the 'Buy Now!' button, then buys the book through Amazon, you get a "click through" fee. I know one author at least who has created a site with a vast database of children's books on it, specifically to generate revenue in this way. Crudely commercial, but I'm told it works.'

After the first hurdle

Your first book has been published. What then? For Susan Davis sales for *The Henry Game* were strong enough for her publisher to come up with a proposal.

'I was asked if I would like to write a sequel, using the same characters and based on the "historical ghost" idea. I already had one in mind, so the second book *Delilah and the Dark Stuff* came very quickly. This was followed by a third book, *Mad, Bad and Totally Dangerous* which was published in July 2004.'

Susan now writes full-time. But she concedes this would not be possible if her husband was not also a breadwinner.

'Advances for children's writers tend to be very small and big discounts to retailers mean smaller or non-existent royalties. I also have to supplement my income by doing editorial work for a literary consultancy. In the past, I have worked as a museum guide, cleaner, care assistant, tourist information assistant, school dinner lady, etc. . . . all fairly mundane jobs which allowed me to keep my brain free for writing.'

A warning not to assume that the first book opens a way to fame and fortune comes from Louise Cooper.

'At the age of nineteen I wrote a fantasy novel (for adults) titled *The Book of Paradise*, and was lucky enough to find an agent willing to take it on. It was published when I was twenty and of course I had all the usual dreams of runaway success – I didn't *quite* get round to swanning into the Rolls-Royce showroom, but it was tempting! And – of course again – the book trickled out on to the market, stayed in a few shops for a few weeks, then vanished without trace!

But that was thirty years ago. I think on the whole that it's now a lot harder for a new writer to break into the market. Yes, there is a tiny minority of first-timers who get the big break and make a fortune, but for everyone else it's probably going to be a protracted struggle. Many publishers, especially in the USA, won't even read a typescript any more, unless it is submitted by an established agent; and I know of quite a few agents who charge for reading unsolicited material. Despite the proliferation of children's books in recent years, there are a great many hurdles for a new writer to overcome and I think that's a great shame because a lot of real talent is probably going unnoticed.'

However, Louise adds an encouraging note:

'After the *Daughter of Storms* trilogy was published, editors from other children's imprints began to approach my agent of the time and ask if I might be interested in writing for them, too. I'm pretty prolific, so, provided that the various books I was writing weren't in direct and obvious competition with each other, I was able to take on commissions for several different publishers.'

Advice for newcomers

We asked our panel, have you any advice to newcomers that has not been covered in earlier questions? Here are the responses.
Catherine and Laurence Anholt:

'Avoid being too clever. The aim is not to prove your abilities as a wordsmith or artist; the aim is to reach children. A good parent does not set out to prove something about themselves to their child – they simply try to foster a creative relationship. An idiosyncratic story about a walking vacuum-cleaner called "Vortex" is not necessarily better than a delightfully funny story about a monkey or a bear. The author's first obligation is TO THE CHILD.'

Susan Davis:

'Aspiring children's writers should be aware that writing for children is not by any means the easy option. Yes, the word count may be a lot shorter than in the average adult novel, but every one of those words has to count. A good story is primary. My main advice would be don't think in terms of writing for children or teenagers, always write primarily for yourself, write the story that intrigues you, the story that has to be written.'

Richard Platt:

'Don't neglect non-fiction. It's the Cinderella of children's publishing, but it's a huge industry, and very much less competitive than fiction. The storybook market for younger children can be very difficult for first-time authors, unless they both write and illustrate. By contrast, if you have a good idea for a non-fiction children's title, and there are no books on this subject already available, there's a good chance that you will be able to find a publisher.

Sell the book *before* you write it, not after. Produce a summary (one to two pages of A4) that briefly describes your idea, listing the main selling points. Include a list of competing titles: be honest about this, but also say why your book is superior. Then approach publishers with this proposal. You may also want to write a sample chapter, but don't try to show how the book might be illustrated or designed, except in the description you provide.

Initially, write about what you know. You won't need to do much research and your enthusiasm will come across in your writing. In the long-term, the attraction of non-fiction writing for children is that there is tremendous variety and you can end up researching weird and wacky subjects about which you know nothing. But to begin with, it's a lot easier to deal with a subject about which you're knowledgeable.

Don't assume that you can cut corners just because kids are the audience. Too many children's non-fiction books are sloppily written and poorly researched. Check every fact with as much care as if you were writing for adults, and keep a record of where you found each piece of information (I use footnotes for this). A year after publication, you're sure to get a letter from the Japanese co-edition publisher querying a statement you've confidently made on page 52. The statement may be true but if you haven't recorded where you found the information, you can spend a day tracking down the source.'

Tony Bradman:

'Surviving as a freelance writer is all about persistence . . . resilience (I've just read a very bad review of one of my books and am working hard at shrugging it off even as I write this!) . . . enthusiasm (you've got to keep coming up with ideas even when you don't feel like it, especially after bad reviews!) and hard work. If you've got any talent, it will come out – and people will always read good, original books!'

Jana Novotny Hunter:

'Read all you can and familiarise yourself with the markets you wish to approach. It is important to target your work at the right publishers. And don't give up. What's wrong for fifty publishers might be the very thing for the fifty-first. Remember, editors are busy people so respect their inability to become your teacher. And no matter how upset you are at the lack of attention your work might achieve, remain polite at all times. The children's book world is small and the same people turn up again and again!'

Louise Cooper:

'The major piece of advice I would give to any aspiring writer is, write what *you* enjoy, about subjects that interest *you*. If an author is excited and involved in his or her story, it shows in the writing; conversely, if the book has been written purely as a hard-nosed commercial exercise, that shows, too, to its detriment. Children get very enthusiastic about the books they read, and demand – quite rightly in my view – the same degree of enthusiasm from their authors. And if you're tempted to try to join in the Rowling/Pullman phenomenon, bear in mind that imitations are very rarely as good as the original!

My second piece of advice is – *never* give up! I was exceptionally lucky to get my first book accepted quite quickly, and I'm well aware that that is the exception rather than the rule. There's a long list of top-selling authors who had to persevere for years before being published, so take comfort from that, and keep writing!'

Criticism

A final word from our editor. We all have a need for constructive criticism but do not assume you will get it from your nearest and dearest. Talking with authors who have made the breakthrough can help, not only with the opening but with all aspects of story-telling. As with any craft, there is at the heart of writing an essential gift, usually made evident by an irrepressible desire to write, no matter how many rejection slips line the walls. But a talent needs the stimulant to grow, which may come from a sympathetic critic or teacher.

This is not an invitation to sign up for one of the writing schools promoted in the small ads of the Sunday press, however. A few may give value for money but the volume of complaints that comes to *The Writer's Handbook* suggests that many more are in for the fast buck, which means signing you up for a year, cash in advance, in the hope that you'll get bored after a couple of dismal lessons but won't press for the money to be returned. University courses usually have more to offer, but even here, care comes before commitment. If a course takes your fancy, check it out with those who have gone before. The ambition to write may not be assisted by lengthy seminars on the meaning of life, a form of self-discovery that some academics seem to think is the sole purpose of literary endeavours. Writers' groups, on the other hand, do come highly recommended if only for the opportunity to talk over problems with those of like mind. This, if any place, is where the honest critic is likely to be found.

Our interviewees

All our interviewees are members of the Society of Authors' Children's Writers and Illustrators Group. Writers who have been offered a contract are eligible to join the Society and membership of the Children's Writers and Illustrators Group is open to writers and illustrators who have had at least one book published by a reputable British publisher, five short stories or more than twenty minutes of material broadcast on national radio or television. You may like to look at their recent publications and websites:

Catherine and Laurence Anholt (www.anholt.co.uk) *Babysitter Bear* (Puffin); *The Magical Garden of Claude Monet* (Frances Lincoln); *The Seriously Silly Stories* (Orchard Books); *Chimp and Zee* (Frances Lincoln); *Jack and the Dreamsack* (Bloomsbury).

Tony Bradman *Voodoo Child (Tales of Terror)* (Egmont Books); *Robin Hood and the Silver Arrow* (Orchard Books); *The Kingfisher Treasury of Pirate Stories* (Kingfisher); *This Little Baby* (Frances Lincoln); *The Orchard Book of Sorcerers and Superheroes* (Orchard Books).

Louise Cooper *Sea Horses* quartet (Puffin); *Butch the Cat-Dog* (Longman-Pearson); *Daughter of Storms* trilogy (Hodder); *Storm Ghost* (Puffin); *Short and Scary!* (Oxford University Press).

Susan Davis *Delilah and the Dark Stuff* (Corgi); *The Henry Game* (Corgi); *The Dinosaur Who Lived in My Backyard* (Puffin).

Jana Novotny Hunter *Read My Lips* (Walker Books); *Little Ones Do!* (Gullane Children's Books); *I Have Feelings* (Frances Lincoln).

Richard Platt *Pirate Diary: The Journal of Jake Carpenter* (Walker Books); *The Vanishing Rainforest* (Frances Lincoln); *Hieroglyphics: Great Inventions and How They Happened* (Kingfisher); *Great Events That Changed the World* (Dorling Kindersley).

Beth Webb (www.bethwebb.co.uk) *Boo Hoo the Ogre* (Appletree Press); *Fleabag and the Ring's End*; *Fleabag and the Fire Cat*; *Fleabag and the Ringfire*; *The Witch of Wookey Hole*; *Foxdown Wood* (all published by Lion).

Children's Bestselling Books 2003

1. *Harry Potter and the Order of the Phoenix* by J.K. Rowling (Bloomsbury) – 2,978,000
2. *Harry Potter and the Goblet of Fire* by J.K. Rowling (Bloomsbury) – 305,000
3. *Harry Potter and the Prisoner of Azkaban* by J.K. Rowling (Bloomsbury) – 299,600
4. *The Beano Annual 2004* (D.C. Thomson) – 230,000
5. *Northern Lights (His Dark Materials)* by Philip Pullman (Scholastic Point) – 199,300
6. *Harry Potter and the Chamber of Secrets* by J.K. Rowling (Bloomsbury) – 168,800
7. *Harry Potter and the Philosopher's Stone* by J.K. Rowling (Bloomsbury) – 168,000
8. *The Subtle Knife (His Dark Materials)* by Philip Pullman (Scholastic Point) – 154,400
9. *The Amber Spyglass (His Dark Materials)* by Philip Pullman (Scholastic Point) – 150,600
10. *Shadowmancer* by G.P. Taylor (Faber & Faber) – 146,200
11. *The Secret Princess Diaries* by Meg Cabot (Macmillan Children's Books) – 141,800
12. *The Wee Free Men* by Terry Prachett (Doubleday Children's Books) – 136,300

13. *The Dandy Book* (D.C. Thomson) – 110,300
14. *Duck's Day Out* by Jez Alborough (Collins) – 108,800
15. *Eagle Strike* by Anthony Wilson (Walker Books) – 108,600
16. *Lola Rose* by Jacqueline Wilson (Doubleday Children's Books) – 108,600
17. *Secrets* by Jacqueline Wilson (Yearling) – 105,900
18. *Tough it Out Tom* by Jenny Oldfield (Hodder Children's Books) – 104,500
19. *Mr Christmas* by Roger Hargreaves (Egmont World) – 102,900
20. *The Last Polar Bears* by Harry Horse (Puffin Books) – 102,200
21. *Midnight* by Jacqueline Wilson (Doubleday Children's Books) – 102,100
22. *Artemis Fowl: The Eternity Code* by Eoin Colfer (Viking Children's Books) – 100,700
23. *The Hostile Hospital (A Series of Unfortunate Events)* by Lemony Snicket (Egmont Books) – 83,800
24. *Showstopper!* by Geraldine McCaughrean (Oxford University Press) – 83,700
25. *Lyra's Oxford* by Philip Pullman (David Fickling Books) – 81,900
26. *Harry Potter and the Chamber of Secrets* by J.K. Rowling (Bloomsbury – Celebratory edition) – 77,800
27. *An Eye for an Eye* by Malorie Blackman (Corgi Juvenile) – 76,700
28. *Harry Potter and the Philosopher's Stone* by J.K. Rowling (Bloomsbury – Celebratory edition) – 75,800
29. *Artemis Fowl* by Eoin Colfer (Puffin Books) – 71,900
30. *Artemis Fowl: The Arctic Incident* by Eoin Colfer (Puffin Books) – 71,500

Classic Children's Authors

Louisa May Alcott   1832–1888
PUBLISHED: Over twenty-five novels including: *Hospital Sketches* (1863); *Little Women* (1868); *Little Men* (1871) and *Jo's Boys and How They Turned Out* (1886).

Hans Christian Andersen   1805–1875
PUBLISHED: *Fairytales Told for Children* (1835); *New Fairytales* (1845); *Wonderful Stories for Children* (1846) and *A Christmas Greeting to My English Friends* (1847). In total Andersen wrote 168 tales and six novels.

J. M. Barrie   1860–1937
PUBLISHED: *Peter and Wendy* (1911) from his stage play *Peter Pan, or The Boy Who Would Not Grow Up* (1904). Other works include: *The Little Minister* (1891); *Sentimental Tommy* (1896); *Tommy and Grizel* (1900); *The Little White Bird* (1902) and numerous stage plays.

L. Frank Baum   1856–1919
PUBLISHED: Fourteen books in the *Wizard of Oz* series commencing with *The Wonderful Wizard of Oz* (1900). Ten Oz related books and a number of books written under the pen names: Floyd Akers; Laura

Bancroft; John Estes Cooke; Capt. Hugh Fitzgerald; Suzanne Metcalf; Schuyler Staunton; Edith Van Dyne and Anonymous.

R. D. Blackmore   1825–1900

PUBLISHED: *Lorna Doone* (1869). Thirteen other novels include *The Maid of Sker* (1872) and *Springhaven* (1887) as well as several volumes of poetry.

Enid Blyton   1897–1968

PUBLISHED: Twenty-one books in *The Famous Five* series; fifteen in *The Secret Seven* series; fifteen in *The Mystery* series; eight in *The Adventures* series; nine in *The School* series; six in the *Malory Towers* series; six in *The Rockingdown Mysteries* series; five in *The Secret* series; five in the *Mary Mouse* series; four in *The Faraway Tree* series; three in *The Wishing Chair* series and numerous books in the *Noddy* series commencing in 1949 with *Noddy Goes to Toyland*. She also published fifteen novels and sixteen collections.

Frances Hodgson Burnett   1849–1924

PUBLISHED: Playwright and novelist who produced over sixty books including several for children. Best known are *Little Lord Fauntleroy* (1886) and *The Secret Garden* (1911).

Lewis Carroll   1832–1898

PUBLISHED: *Alice's Adventures in Wonderland* (1865); *Through the Looking Glass and What Alice Found There* (1871); *The Hunting of the Snark* (1876); *The Wasp in a Wig* (1877); *A Tangled Tale* (1885); *The Nursery Alice* (1889) and *Sylvie and Bruno* (1889).

Richmal Crompton   1890–1969

PUBLISHED: Thirty-nine books in the *Just William* series. The first, *Just William*, was published in 1922. Her last book, *William and the*

Lawless, was completed by her niece and published after her death in 1970.

Roald Dahl   1916–1990

PUBLISHED: *The Gremlins* (1943); *Sometime Never: A Fable for Supermen* (1948); *James and the Giant Peach* (1961); *Charlie and the Chocolate Factory* (1964); *The Magic Finger* (1966); *Fantastic Mr Fox* (1970); *Charlie and the Great Glass Elevator* (1972); *Danny, The Champion of the World* (1975); *The Enormous Crocodile* (1976); *My Uncle Oswald* (1979); *The Twits* (1980); *George's Marvellous Medicine* (1981); *The BFG* (1982); *Dirty Beasts* (1983); *The Witches* (1983); *The Giraffe and the Pelly and Me* (1985); *Going Solo* (1986); *Matilda* (1988); *Esio Troat* (1989); *Rhyme Stew* (1989); *The Great Switcheroo* (1990); *The Minpins* (1991); *The Vicar of Nibbleswicke* (1991); *My Year* (1993) and *The Mildenhall Treasure* (1999). Dahl also wrote a number of adult books and a number of his children's books have been made into films.

Daniel Defoe   1660–1731

PUBLISHED: *Robinson Crusoe* (1719); *The Further Adventures of Robinson Crusoe* (1719) and *The Serious Reflections of Robinson Crusoe* (1729). Included in his adult novels are *Moll Flanders* (1722) and *Roxana* (1724).

Kenneth Grahame   1859–1932

PUBLISHED: *The Wind in the Willows* (1908). Two earlier books *The Golden Days* (1895) and its sequel *Dream Days* (1898) were also written for children. Grahame also compiled *The Cambridge Book of Poetry for Young People* (1916).

Grimm Brothers
(Jacob Grimm 1785–1863 and Wilhelm Grimm 1786–1859)

PUBLISHED: Various anthologies of folktales and legends in 1812,

1819, 1822, 1837, 1840, 1843, 1850 and 1857. The final edition consists of 200 stories and ten legends. This version was the basis for future editions and translations published posthumously.

Roger Hargreaves   1935–1988
PUBLISHED: Forty-three books in the *Mr Men* series of which the first, *Mr Tickle*, was published in 1971. The *Little Miss* series, of which there were thirty, was started in 1981. Hargreaves also drew all the illustrations. Following his death in 1988 his son, Adam, has continued to write and illustrate new stories around the old characters.

Hergé (Georges Rémi)   1907–1983
PUBLISHED: Twenty-four books in *The Adventures of Tintin* series. The first, *The Adventures of Tintin in the Land of the Soviets*, was published in 1930 and the last, *Tintin and the Alpharts*, was published, after his death, in 1986.

Thomas Hughes   1822–1896
PUBLISHED: *Tom Brown's Schooldays* (1857). The sequel *Tom Brown at Oxford* did not achieve the same success. His only other novel *The Scouring of the White Horse* appeared in 1859.

Tove Jansson   1914–2001
PUBLISHED: Nine books about the Moomintrolls which she also illustrated. The first, *The Little Trolls and the Great Flood*, appeared in 1945 and the last, *Moominvalley in November*, in 1970. They have been translated in thirty-four languages and dramatised for theatre, opera, film, radio and TV.

Captain W. E. Johns   1893–1968
PUBLISHED: Ninety-six *Biggles* books between 1932 and 1970 with

an additional six omnibus editions plus two further books published in the 1990s. Eleven books in the *Worrals* series between 1941 and 1950. Ten *Gimlet* books published between 1943 and 1954. Six *Steeley* books between 1936 and 1939, eight children's books between 1938 and 1960 and twelve adult books between 1922 and 1960 as well as numerous short stories.

Rudyard Kipling   1865–1936

PUBLISHED: *The Jungle Book* (1894), *The Second Jungle Book* (1895), the *Just So Stories* (1902), *Puck of Pook's Hall* (1906) and his novel about India, *Kim* (1901).

C. S. Lewis   1898–1963

PUBLISHED: Best known for his seven *Chronicles of Narnia*: *The Lion, the Witch and the Wardrobe* (1950); *Prince Caspian* (1951); *The Voyage of the Dawn Treader* (1952); *The Silver Chair* (1953); *The Horse and His Boy* (1954); *The Last Battle* (1956) and *The Magician's Nephew* (1959).

A. A. Milne   1882–1956

PUBLISHED: Four books in the *Pooh* series. The first, a collection of verse, *When We Were Very Young* (1924), was followed by *Winnie-the-Pooh* (1926). Another collection of verse, *Now We Are Six* was published in 1927 with the fourth book, *Pooh Corner*, appearing in 1928. Milne also wrote a number of plays and novels.

L.M. Montgomery   1874–1942

PUBLISHED: Ten books in the *Anne* series commencing with *Anne of Green Gables* (1908) and ending with *Anne of Ingleside* (1939). Three books were published about another young girl called Emily and two about the King Family. Montgomery wrote several adult novels and collections of poems. Publication of her diaries (1889–1942) began in 1985.

Beatrix Potter 1886–1943

PUBLISHED: Twenty-three titles in the *Peter Rabbit* series commencing in 1902 with *The Tale of Peter Rabbit* and culminating in 1930 with *The Tale of Little Pig Robinson*.

Arthur Ransome 1884–1967

PUBLISHED: *Swallows and Amazons* (1930) was the first in a series of twelve novels for children. The last book, *Great Northern?* (1947), was followed forty years later by the publication of a posthumous thirteenth novel, *Coots in the North and Other Stories*, based on an uncompleted manuscript.

Antoine de Saint-Exupéry 1900–1944

PUBLISHED: *The Little Prince* (1943) plus six other novels.

Richard Scarry 1919–1994

PUBLISHED: *The Two Little Miners* in 1948 followed by five other children's books. His first book as an author and illustrator, *The Best Word Book Ever*, was published in 1963 and over the next thirty years he produced about four or five titles a year. Best known in his output of over three hundred books are: *Busy, Busy World* (1965); *Storybook Dictionary* (1967) and *Biggest Word Book Ever* (1985).

Dr Seuss 1904–1991

PUBLISHED: Having spent many years as a cartoonist and illustrator, Seuss's first children's book, *I Saw It on Mulberry Street* was published in 1937. His early successes include *The 500 Hats of Bartholomew Cubbins* (1938), *Horton Hatches an Egg* (1940) and *If I Ran a Circus* (1955). *The Cat in a Hat* (1957) established his reputation and *Green Eggs and Ham* (1960) became his most popular book.

Anna Sewell   1820–1878
PUBLISHED: *Black Beauty* (1877).

Robert Louis Stevenson   1850–1894
PUBLISHED: Numerous novels, essays and collections of poetry. His adventure books such as *Treasure Island* (1883); *Kidnapped* (1886); *The Master of Ballantrae* (1889) and *Catriona* (1893) are enjoyed by children and adults alike. *A Child's Garden of Verses* was published in 1885.

J. R. R. Tolkien   1892–1973
PUBLISHED: *The Hobbit* (1937), *The Lord of the Rings* (1954–55) and *The Silmarillion* (1977).

Mark Twain   1835–1910
PUBLISHED: Around ten novels including three books which drew on his childhood experiences in the Mississippi: *The Adventures of Tom Sawyer* (1876); *Life on the Mississippi* (1883) and *The Adventures of Huckleberry Finn* (1885).

Contemporary Children's Writers

Jez Alborough was born in Kingston upon Thames, Surrey, in 1959. After attending art school in Norwich, he worked as an editorial illustrator before starting to write. His first book *Bare Bear* was published in 1984 by Ernest Benn and was runner-up for the 1985 Mother Goose Award. His career took off with the publication of *Where's My Teddy?* (Walker Books, 1994). Titles include the following for Walker Books: *Eddy & Bear Sticker Book* (1993); *Cuddly Dudley* (1994); *It's the Bear!* (1996); *Hello Beaky!* (1998); *Washing Line* (1998); *Something at the Letterbox* (1998); *Watch Out! Big Bro's Coming!* (1999); *Ice-Cream Bear* (1999); *Washing Line – Maths Together* (1999); *My Friend Bear* (2000); *Where's My Teddy Mini* (2001); *Hug* (2002); *Best Things in Life* (2002); *Latest Craze* (2002); *Brave Knights* (2002); *Eddy & Bear Silly Sticker Book* (2003) and *Some Dogs Do* (2003). Books published by HarperCollins include: *Balloon* (1999); *Duck in the Truck* (1999); *Fix–it Duck* (2001); *Captain Duck* (2002); *Guess What Happened at School Today* (2003) and *Duck's Day Out –* board book (2004). Alborough uses rhyme and humour, coupled with his own unique illustrations. A frequent guest at storytelling events, Alborough also devises classroom 'activity' worksheets for many of his titles.

'Some people write children's books for their own children but I don't have any children. I write for the child I was.'

David Almond (www.davidalmond.com) was born in Newcastle and raised in Felling-on-Tyne. After graduating with a degree in English and American Literature from the University of East Anglia, David trained to be a teacher and spent five years in a primary school in Gateshead. While he was there he began to write short stories. After he resigned to concentrate on his writing, Almond's debut children's novel, *Skellig*, was published by Hodder in 1998 and won both the Whitbread Book of the Year Award and the Carnegie Medal. He adapted it for the stage and it was produced at the Young Vic in 2003/04. *Skellig* was followed by *Kit's Wilderness* (Hodder, 1999), *Heaven Eyes* (Hodder, 2000) and *Secret Heart* (Hodder, 2001). His latest book, *The Fire-Eaters* (Hodder, 2003), won the Nestlé Smarties Book Prize 2003 and the Whitbread Children's Book of the Year Award 2003. It was also shortlisted for the *Guardian* Children's Fiction Award.

David's advice for writers:

'Writing can be hard, but it's also a kind of play. I do lots of fast scribbling in notebooks. I allow myself to write lots of rubbish and am often surprised by what comes out of my head. When I start to put a story together, I try to stay relaxed and to allow the story to grow organically. I put the story together, sentence by sentence, chapter by chapter and try not to worry too much about how it will end.'

Catherine and Laurence Anholt (www.anholt.co.uk) are a husband and wife team. Author (Laurence) and illustrator (Catherine) have over seventy titles in print and have won numerous awards including the 2001 Nestlé Smarties Gold Award (0–5yrs) for *Chimp and*

Zee (Frances Lincoln, 2001). Laurence also received this award (6–8 yrs) in 1999 for *Snow White and the Seven Aliens* (Orchard Books). Their first book *Truffles* was published in 1984. Laurence has illustrated a number of his own titles including a series about great artists which grew out of his exposure to art during his early childhood in Holland. Titles, all published by Frances Lincoln, include: *Camille and the Sunflowers* (1994); *Degas and the Little Dancer* (1996) and *Picasso and the Girl with a Ponytail* (1998). Supporters of numerous literacy and reading organisations, they were commissioned by the British government to produce a booklet *Babies Love Books* for the Bookstart scheme. The Anholts have also produced two other series of books – the *Seriously Silly* series and *The One and Only* series.

Their advice:

'You should aim to come up with something which is original, contemporary, international/universal, politically correct, passionate, personal, poetic, inventive, theatrical, exciting, emotional, optimistic, inspiring . . . it's as easy as that!'

Malorie Blackman (www.malorieblackman.co.uk) was born in London in 1962. She had a variety of jobs, including one as a database manager for Reuters, which involved a lot of travel in Europe and the United States. Her first novel, *Hacker*, published by Transworld in 1991, won two major awards in 1994 – The WH Smith's Mind Boggling Book Award and the *Young Telegraph*/Gimme 5 Children's Book of the Year Award. Other award-winning titles include *Thief!* (Doubleday, 1995), *A.N.T.I.D.O.T.E.* (Doubleday, 1997) and *Pig-Heart Boy* (Doubleday, 1997). In 2002 – along with three other awards – Blackman received the Red House Children's Book Award for *Noughts and Crosses* (Doubleday, 2001). The second book in this trilogy *Knife Edge* (Doubleday, 2004), will be followed by the third scheduled for 2005. Books written for younger readers include five in the *Betsey Biggalow* series (Piccadilly Press, 1992), *Whizziwig* (Viking, 1995), and *Animal Avengers* (Mammoth, 1999). Picture books include *Marty Monster* (Tamarind Ltd, 1999), *I Want a Cuddle* (Orchard, 2001) and *Jessica Strange* (Hodder, 2002). Her main tips for writers are, to keep a diary, to write down your thoughts and feelings about things, to find your own way of expressing yourself, and to read.

'In my opinion if you don't read, you can't write.'

Quentin Blake was born in 1932. Acknowledged as one of Britain's best and most successful illustrators, he is also the author of over twenty-five children's books. He has collaborated with writers such as Michael Rosen, Russell Hoban and Joan Aiken, but his most famous partnership is with Roald Dahl, of which *The BFG*, *Matilda*, *The Witches* and *Charlie and the Chocolate Factory* are the best known. Blake's first drawing was published in *Punch* when he was sixteen. After reading English at Cambridge he did a postgraduate teaching course at the University of London and attended life classes at Chelsea Art School. As well as teaching illustration at the Royal College of Art for over twenty years, Blake continued to draw for *Punch*, *The Spectator* and other magazines. The first book he illustrated, in 1960, was *A Drink of Water* by John Yeoman. The first book he wrote and illustrated, *Patrick*, was published in 1968. In 1999 he was appointed the first Children's Laureate and, in 2002, produced *Laureate's Progress* (Jonathan Cape) which recorded his two-year tenure. The *Guardian* described him as 'a national institution'. Books written and illustrated by Blake include: *Angelo* (Jonathan Cape, 1970); *Mrs Armitage on Wheels* (Jonathan Cape, 1987); *Mrs Armitage and the Big Wave* (Red Fox, 1988); *Mister Magnolia* (Hutchinson, 1999); *Zagazoo* (Red Fox, 2000); *Loveykins* (Jonathan Cape, 2002) and

Mrs Armitage, Queen of the Road (Jonathan Cape, 2003). In 2002, Red Fox published *A Sailing Boat in the Sky* – the result of a unique collaboration with 1,800 French-speaking children. Quentin Blake has won the 1981 Children's Book Award, the Kate Greenaway Medal, the Whitbread Award, the Hans Christian Andersen Award for Illustration and the Nestlé Smarties Award. In 1988 he was awarded the OBE.

'Blake is beyond brilliant. He's anarchic, moral, infinitely subversive, sometimes vicious, socially acute, sparse when he has to be, exuberantly lavish in the detail when he feels like it. He can tell wonderful stories without a single word, but his partnership with Roald Dahl was made in heaven. Or somewhere. The diabolic ingenuity of Dahl came into its own only when he wrote for children. In conjunction with Blake, there was a kind of alchemy. I've never met a child who didn't love Quentin Blake.' Melanie McDonagh, *Daily Telegraph*

Michael Bond was born in Newbury in 1926. Educated at Presentation College, Reading, he served in both the Royal Air Force and the Middlesex Regiment during World War II. His first short story was sold to the magazine *London Opinion* in 1945, but it was not until 1958 that his first book, *A Bear Called Paddington*, was published by William Collins & Sons – now HarperCollins Publishers. At this time he was working as a cameraman for the BBC, but by 1967 his *Paddington* books were such a success he left to become a full-time writer. The main titles that followed, all illustrated by Peggy Fortnum and published by Collins, are: *More About Paddington* (1959); *Paddington Helps Out* (1960); *Paddington Abroad* (1961); *Paddington at Large* (1962); *Paddington Marches On* (1964); *Paddington at Work* (1966); *Paddington Goes to Town* (1968); *Paddington Takes the Air* (1970); *Paddington on Top* (1974) and *Paddington Takes the Test* (1979). In the 1970s Bond created a TV children's series *The Herbs* which ran to forty-five episodes. His other series of books for children, aged seven to nine, is about a guinea pig, *Olga da Polga*. Titles in this series are published by Oxford University Press and include *The Tales of Olga da Polga, Olga Meets Her Match, Olga Takes Charge, Olga Carries On, Olga Moves House* (2001) *and Olga Follows Her Nose* (2002). In total Bond has written over 150 books, and in 1997 was awarded the OBE.

Raymond Briggs was born in London in 1934. Educated at Rutlish Grammar School in Merton, he went on to study art at Wimbledon Art School and the Slade School of Fine Art from which he graduated in 1957. He had already worked as a commercial artist in advertising prior to leaving the Slade. He has twice won the Kate Greenaway Medal – first for *His Mother Goose Treasury* in 1966 (Hamish Hamilton) and later for *Father Christmas* in 1973 (Hamish Hamilton). *Fungus the Bogeyman* (Hamish Hamilton, 1977) preceded his best-known book *The Snowman* (Hamish Hamilton, 1978). *The Snowman* was made into an animated film in 1982 and also appears regularly in a stage version at Christmas. Another favourite with children, *The Bear* (Hamish Hamilton, 1994), has also been filmed, as has his adult book – the satire on nuclear war *When the Wind Blows* (Hamish Hamilton, 1982). Later books for children include *Ethel and Ernest* (Jonathan Cape, 1998), for which Briggs won the Illustrated Book of the Year Award, and *UG – Boy Genius of the Stone Age* (Jonathan Cape, 2001).

'Most of my ideas seem to be based on a simple premise; let's assume that something imaginary – a snowman, a bogeyman, a Father Christmas – is wholly real and proceed logically from there.'

Melvin Burgess was born in 1954. By his own admission he was a dreamy child and not academically bright, although he liked English.

On moving from Sussex to Reading he attended a new comprehensive school and achieved two A-levels in English and Biology. He then got a job as a journalist on a local paper, but after the six-month training course decided that he wanted to write books, and that no other career would suffice. During the next fifteen years he moved to Bristol, where he enjoyed the racial and cultural mix in the inner city, earning his living in a series of casual jobs while continuing to write, 'without success'. Aged thirty-five, he moved to London where in 1990 his first book *The Cry of the Wolf* was published by Andersen Press and shortlisted for the Carnegie Medal. The following have since been published by Andersen Press unless otherwise indicated: *Burning Issy* (1992); *An Angel for May* (1992), shortlisted for the Carnegie Medal; *The Baby and Fly Pie* (1993), shortlisted for the Carnegie Medal; *Loving April* (1994); *The Earth Giant* (1995) and *Tiger Tiger* (1996). His next book *Junk* (1996) – based largely on his experiences in Bristol – caused a commotion as it deals with teenage heroin addiction. It won the *Guardian* Fiction Prize and the Carnegie Medal. Next came: *Kite* (1997); *The Copper Treasure* (A&C Black, 1998); *Bloodtide* (1999); *The Ghost Behind the Wall* (2000), shortlisted for the Carnegie Medal; *The Birdman*, his first picture book, (2000) and *Lady – My Life as a Bitch* (2002). *Lady* – the story of a teenage girl who drinks, smokes, has casual sex and turns into a dog – also courted huge controversy. Burgess's reputation is now well established as someone not afraid to deal with tough subjects such as homelessness, disability, child abuse, witchcraft, sex and drugs.

Burgess's latest book *Doing It* (2003) received the following review:

> 'I think that Melvin's treatment of that whole confusing scenario of being a teenager – racing hormones, peer pressure, trying to "find" yourself as an individual and simply trying to enjoy your teen years – is, as ever, brilliant.' Caroline Horn, *The Bookseller*

Meg Cabot (www.megcabot.com) was born in Indiana, USA. She obtained a fine arts degree from Indiana University before moving to New York City to pursue a career in freelance illustration. This was soon abandoned to concentrate on writing. Her first books – historical adult romances – were written under the name of Patricia Cabot. In October 2000, her first teenage novel *The Princess Diaries* was written under her own name and published by HarperCollins. Following this, Pocket Books published *The Mediator: Shadowland* (2000), the first in her series of teenage supernatural novels, written under the name of Jenny Carroll. Also under the pseudonym of Jenny Carroll, Cabot has written the series *1–800-WHERE-R-YOU*. The first of these, subtitled *When Lightning Strikes*, was published by Pocket Books in 2000. The five volumes of *The Princess Diaries* are published by HarperCollins, the five novels in *The Mediator* series are published by Pocket Books and written as Jenny Carroll – apart from the latest title *Haunted: A Tale of the Mediator* (HarperCollins, 2003) – which was published under her own name. Two historical teenage romances were published by HarperCollins in 2002 and 2003 respectively under the overall title of *An Avon Romance*. Her latest book *Teen Idol* is a contemporary teenage novel (Harper-Collins, 2004). The film of *The Princess Diaries* has been a box office success both in the UK and the USA. Pan Macmillan is the outlet for her books in the UK. Her advice to young writers:

> 'Write the kinds of stories you like to read. If you don't love what you're writing, no one else will, either.'

Eoin Colfer was born in Wexford, Ireland in 1965. He attended the local primary school where his father was a teacher and historian, and his mother, a drama teacher and actress. From an early age he had a keen interest in writing and illustrating. On leaving Dublin University, he qualified as a primary teacher in 1986 and returned to Wexford. Following his marriage in 1991, he and his wife left Ireland and spent the next four years teaching in Saudi Arabia, Tunisia and Italy. On returning to Wexford, Colfer continued to write and his first book *Benny and Omar* (O'Brien Press, 1998) relates the adventures of an Irish boy and his Tunisian friend. *Benny and Babe* followed in 1999 along with the O'Brien Flyers series: *Going Potty* (1999); *Ed's Funny Feet* (2000) and *Ed's Bed* (2001). He sent his next book *Artemis Fowl* to the UK literary agent, Sophie Hicks and, on publication by Puffin Books in 2001, it became a bestseller, winning the British Book Awards Children's Book of the Year Award. The sequel *Artemis Fowl: The Arctic Incident* (Puffin, 2002) was followed by *Artemis Fowl: The Eternity Code* (Puffin, 2003). Colfer describes his books as: '*Die Hard* with fairies.'

'Artemis Fowl is absolutely brilliant. Hardcase leprechauns, elves with attitude, fairies that are anything but and a troll to make Voldemort look like a wuss: the fairytale has been redefined!' Luise Pattinson, *The Book House*

Lynley Dodd was born in 1941 in New Zealand. On graduating from art school and after gaining a teaching diploma, she became an art teacher. Her literary career started as an illustrator for other authors before moving on to produce her own stories and drawings. Early publications include: *The Nickle Nackle Tree* (1976); *The Smallest Turtle* (1982) and *The Appletree* (1983). In 1983 *Hairy Maclary from Donaldson's Dairy* was published and brought widespread recognition. It was followed by: *Hairy Maclary's Bone* (1984); *Hairy Maclary Scattercat* (1985); *Hairy Maclary's Caterwaul Caper* (1987); *Hairy Maclairy's Rumpus at the Vet* (1989); *Hairy Maclary's Showbusiness* (1991); *Hairy Maclary, Sit* (1996); and *Hairy Maclary and Zachary Quack* (1996). In 1990 she produced the first of her *Slinky Malinki* books, followed in 1992 by *Slinky Malinki Open the Door*, and in 1998 by *Slinky Malinki Catflaps*. Dodd has produced several one-off titles such as *Hedgehog Howdedo* (2000) and *Scarface Claw* (2001). She has written three books about a dachshund – *Schnitzel von Krumm's Basketwork* (1994), *Schnitzel von Krumm, Forget-me-Not* (1996) and *Schnitzel von Krumm, Dogs Never Climb* (2002). In the UK the majority of these books are published by Penguin. In New Zealand, Dodd has won many awards, several times over, including the Children's Picture Book of the Year Award. In 2002 she was awarded a Distinguished Companions of the New Zealand Order of Merit.

> 'I learned to rely on my own resources and imagination. Looking back, I don't even remember having been bored. When I wasn't involved in endless flights of imagination outdoors with any available children, I was reading avidly or drawing.'

Julia Donaldson was born in North London. After graduating from Bristol University she worked for the BBC for several years, writing songs for children's television. One of the songs became the book *A Squash and a Squeeze* with illustrations by the German illustrator, Axel Scheffler. This partnership led to many successful publications, notably *The Gruffalo* published in 1999 by Macmillan Children's Books. In the same year it won the Nestlé Smarties Gold Award (0–5 yrs) and was also judged the Best Book to Read Aloud at the *Blue Peter* Awards in 2000. Also by Donaldson and Scheffler and published by Macmillan are: *Monkey Puzzle* (2000); *Room on the Broom* (2001) – winner of the 2003 *Blue Peter* Best Book to Read Aloud Award; *The Smartest Giant in Town* (2002); *The Snail and the Whale* (2003) and *Jingle, Jangle, Jungle* (Campbell Books, 2003). Other publications include *The Dinosaur's Diary* (Young Puffin Books, 2002), *Night Monkey, Day Monkey* (Egmont Books, 2002), *Spinderella* (Egmont Books, 2002), *Tales from Acorn Wood* (Macmillan, 2002), *The Magic Paintbrush* (Macmillan, 2003); and *Princess Mirror-Belle* (Macmillan, 2003).

Donaldson now lives in Glasgow where she continues to write, and visits schools and libraries. She also holds drama and storytelling workshops.

Anne Fine was born in 1947. She attended Northampton High School for Girls and studied history and politics at the University of Warwick. Since her first novel for young teenagers *The Summer House Loon* was published by Mammoth in 1978, Fine has written over forty books for children of all ages and won numerous awards, both in the UK and abroad. In 1989 she won the Nestlé Smarties Prize (6–8 yrs) for *Bill's New Frock* (Methuen). The following year she won both the *Guardian* Children's Fiction Prize and the Carnegie Medal for *Goggle-Eyes* (Puffin, 1989). Both have since been adapted for television by the BBC. In 1990 and 1993 she was voted *Publishing News'* Children's Author of the Year. She won the Carnegie Medal again in 1993, as well as the Whitbread Children's Book of the Year Award, for *Flour Babies* (Puffin, 1992). Fine was awarded a second Whitbread in 1996 for *The Tulip Touch* (Puffin, 1996). In May 2001 she became the second Children's Laureate, a post she held for two years.

> 'Her copious and often comical dialogue rings entirely true (a rare gift), while out of the ephemera of everyday life she constructs a tale of lasting power.' *The Financial Times*

Anthony Horowitz was born in London in 1955. Following boarding school in Harrow, he attended York University, and wrote his first book *Enter Frederick K. Bower* (Arlington Books, 1978) at the age of twenty-three. His name is largely associated with murder mysteries for television, having created the series *Midsomer Murders*, *Murder in Mind* and *Foyle's Law*. However, he has also gained a considerable reputation for his many children's books. In 2003 he won the Red House Children's Book Award for *Skeleton Key* (Walker Books, 2002), the third novel in his Alex Rider series about a teenage spy. The others, all published by Walker Books, are *Stormbreaker* (2000), *Point Blanc* (2002), *Eagle Strike* (2003) and *Scorpia* (2004). The Diamond Brothers feature in a series of mystery novels commencing in 1986 with *The Falcon's Malteser* (Armada, 1986). Others in the series include: *Public Enemy Number Two* (Collins, 1987); *South by South East* (Lions, 1991); *The French Confection* (Walker Books, 2002); *The Blurred Man* (Walker Books, 2002) and *I Know What You Did Last Wednesday* (Walker Books, 2002). *The Groosham Grange* (Methuen, 1988) was followed by *The Unholy Grail* (Methuen, 1991) and *Return to Groosham Grange* (Walker Books, 2003). Horowitz has over sixteen individual titles published by Walker Books and one, *Myths and Legends*, published by Kingfisher in 1993.

His advice for beginners:

'Never give up. Never be put off by a rejection. Remember that most publishers aren't as clever as you.'

Harry Horse, otherwise known as Richard Horne, was born in Coventry in 1960 and currently lives in Edinburgh. He was training to be a lawyer when he decided he wanted to pursue a career as an illustrator, and moved to Scotland. He made his debut as an author and illustrator in 1983 with *The Opogogo – My Journey with the Loch Ness Monster*. Between 1987 and 1992 he was the political cartoonist for *Scotland on Sunday* and his illustrations have also appeared in the *Independent*, the *Observer*, *Vox* and the *New Yorker*. In 1992 Horse sent *The Last Polar Bears* to Penguin Children's Books. The publisher, Philippa Milnes-Smith, recognising his talent as a gifted writer and illustrator, published it in 1993. In the same year it was shortlisted for the Children's Book Award and has since been developed into a thirty-minute animated film. In 1998 he won the Gold Nestlé

Smarties Award (6–8 yrs) for *The Last Gold Diggers* (Puffin, 1998) and in 2003 he was the recipient of their Silver Award for *The Last Castaways* (Puffin, 2003). *Little Rabbit Lost* (Puffin, 2002) won the 2003 Scottish Arts Council's Children's Book of the Year Award. The books in *The Last . . .* series, including *The Last Cowboys* (Puffin, 1999) were inspired by his dog, Roo. Publications by Walker Books include: *A Friend for Little Bear* (1996) and *Higglety Pigglety Pop and Other Funny Poems* (2002). Harry Horse has also illustrated for other authors including: Dick King-Smith, Vivian French, John Wallace and Stuart McDonald.

'An inventive, gentle writer.' *Scotland on Sunday*

Shirley Hughes was born in Holylake, near Liverpool, in 1927. She was educated at West Kirby High School and then went on to study drawing and costume design at the Liverpool School of Art and the Ruskin School, Oxford. Her ability to draw children in a naturalistic style was soon recognised, gaining her a commission from *Collins Children's Magazine*. Having moved to London, Hughes married and had three children. During the 1950s and '60s she mainly illustrated other authors' books, notably *My Naughty Little Sister* (Methuen, 1969) by Dorothy Edwards. From the 1970s onwards she has written and illustrated over fifty books, and in 1977 won the Kate Greenaway Medal for *Dogger* (Bodley Head). Her best-loved books are about the characters Lucy and Tom, and Alfie and Annie Rose as well as a series of books about the people who live in Trotter Street. Titles published by Gollancz (now part of Orion Children's) include: *Lucy and Tom's Day* (1960); *Lucy and Tom go to School* (1973); *Lucy and Tom at the Seaside* (1976); *Lucy and Tom's Christmas* (1981) and *Lucy and Tom's ABC* (1984). Published by The Bodley Head (now part of Random House Children's Books): *The Trouble with Jack* (1970); *Sally's Secret* (1973); *Clothes* (1974); *Helpers* (1975); *Up and Up*

(1979); *Moving Molly* (1978); *Alfie Gets in First* (1981); *Alfie's Feet* (1982); *Alfie Gives a Hand* (1983); *An Evening at Alfie's* (1984); *Chips and Jessie* (1985); *Big Alfie and Annie Rose Storybook* (1988); *Stories by the Firelight* (1993); *Enchantment in the Garden* (1996); *Ella's Big Chance* (2003). Published by Walker Brothers, titles include: *All Shapes and Sizes* (1986); *The Big Concrete Lorry, A Tale of Trotter Street* (1989); *Bouncing* (1993); *Hiding* (1994); *Chatting* (1994); *Playing* (1997) and *Being Together* (1997). Other titles include: *George: The Babysitter* (Simon & Schuster, 1978); *When We Went to the Park* (HarperCollins, 1985); *Angel Mae, A Tale of Trotter Street* (HarperCollins, 1989) and *It's Too Frightening for Me* (Young Puffin, 1980). Hughes won the Eleanor Farjeon Award in 1984 and in 1999 was awarded an OBE.

'The root of good illustration is good draftsmanship. If you cannot draw, your colours won't work. It is an intellectual activity, but it is hard to convince people of that here in England, where we are terribly word-oriented.' *The Lady*

Mick Inkpen was born in Romford, Essex, in 1952. He began his career as a graphic designer, having declined a place in 1969 to study English at Cambridge University. During this period he met Nick Butterworth, and together they developed a cartoon strip for the *Sunday Express* magazine called *Upney Junction*. This later became a series of picture books about a gang of mice. With Butterworth he produced over thirty different titles. His first solo title for Hodder Children's Books was *One Bear at Bedtime* (1987), but it was with the publication of *The Blue Balloon* (Hodder, 1989) – in which the dog Kipper appeared for the first time – that Inkpen really became established as a children's author in his own right. *Kipper* (1991) was the first in a long-running series of successful titles, now sold worldwide. In 2001 Inkpen won the Nestlé Smarties Silver Award (0–5 yrs) for *Kipper's A-Z* and in 1998 *Kipper* won a BAFTA for the best-animated children's film. Likewise the *Wibbly Pig* books, first published in 1995, continue to be an international success. Titles in this series, all published by Hodder in 1995, include: *Wibbly Pig Can Dance; Wibbly Pig Can Make a Tent; Wibbly Pig is Happy; Wibbly Pig is Upset; Wibbly Pig Likes Bananas; Wibbly Pig Makes Pictures* and *Wibbly Pig Opens his Presents*. Most recent titles for Hodder are: *Blue Nose Island: Ploo and the Terrible Gnobbler* (2003) and *Is It Bedtime Wibbly Pig?*(2004). Other awards include: the 1991 Children's Book Award for *Threadbear* (Hodder, 1990) and the 1992 Illustrated Children's Book of the Year Award for *Penguin Small*. In 1993 he was shortlisted in the same category for *Lullabyhullabaloo!*, and in 1994 for Children's Author of the Year. According to the Public Lending Right's statistics for 2002–03, Inkpen was the fifth most borrowed author from public libraries. He continues to live in Essex and has two children.

> 'Without the experience of having children of my own I doubt that I would have been capable of writing effectively for children. And yet it's true that good work really springs from trying to please yourself.'

Brian Jacques was born in Liverpool in 1939. On leaving school he became a merchant seaman for several years before returning to Liverpool. A variety of jobs – lorry driver, bus driver and policeman – ensued before the start of a life in the creative arts as a folk singer, stand-up comedian and playwright. His career as a children's author began with the *Redwall* series, about a band of mice protecting a monastery from evil rats. Jacques wrote the first of these for the children at The Royal Wavertree School for the Blind. There are now over sixteen books in the series, which was originally published by Hutchinson – now part of the Random House Group. Titles include: *Redwall* (1986); *Mossflower* (1988); *Mattimeo* (1990); *Mariel of Redmond* (1991); *Salamandastron* (1992); *Martin the Warrior* (1993); *The Bellmaker* (1994); *Outcast of Redwall* (1995); *The Pearls of Lutra* (1997);

The Long Patrol (1997); *Marlfox* (1998); *The Legend of Luke* (1999); *Redwall Friend and Foe* (2000); *Lord Brocktree* (2000); *Tribes of Redwall – Badgers* (2001); *The Taggerung* (2001); *A Redwall Winter's Tale* (2001); *The Tribes of Redwall – Otters* (2002); *Triss* (2002); *The Tribes of Redwall – Mice* (2003) and *Loamhedge* (2003). Jacques continues to live and write in Liverpool as well as presenting his own programme on Radio Merseyside.

> 'I have always been a keen writer. Even at school it was my one real forte. There is not a day when a person suddenly becomes an *author*. Over many years of writing for different media a style develops and the ease and comfort of writing what you really know about is very important to this development.' *Young Writer* magazine, 1997

Dick King-Smith was born in Gloucestershire in 1922. During World War II he served in the Grenadier Guards before returning to Gloucestershire, where he spent the next twenty years farming. King-Smith then trained to become a primary school teacher. During his seven years as a teacher he wrote his first four books, of which *The Fox Busters* was the first to be published (Crown Books, 1975). Since then he has written hundreds of books, mostly published by the Random House Group, based on his love of the countryside and animals. *Babe: The Gallant Pig* (Yearling, 1983) was made into the hit film *Babe* in 1995. More recent publications include: *Horse Pie* (Corgi Juvenile, 1994); *Harriet's Hare* (Doubleday, 1995) – which won the overall Red House Children's Book Award in the same year; *All Because of Jackson* (Doubleday, 1995) – won the Bronze Nestlé Smarties Award 1997; *Funny Frank* (Doubleday, 2001); *Titus Rules OK!* (Doubleday, 2002); *The Adventurous Snail* (Doubleday, 2003); *Aristotle* (Walker Books, 2003); *Just Binnie* (Puffin, 2004) and *Here Comes Sophie* (Walker Books, 2004). In 1992 he was voted the British Books Author of the Year.

'Writing my books is like handing out presents. Giving children pleasure gives you a wonderful sort of Father Christmassy feeling.'
BBC Gloucestershire website: www.bbc.co.uk/gloucestershire

Michael Morpurgo was born in St Albans in 1943 and was educated at Kings Canterbury, Sandhurst, and Kings College, London. He became a teacher following a brief spell in the army. In 1976 he and his wife moved to Devon to set up the charity, Farms for City Children. Two more have been established in Wales and Gloucestershire where children from inner-city schools can spend time in a farm environment. His first picture book for Collins, *Sam's Duck* (1996), is based on the first farm. Morpurgo has written over sixty books, his first title, *Long Way Home*, being published by Macmillan in 1975. Translated into over twenty languages, his books have also been adapted for the theatre, and five have been made into films including *Why the Whales Came* (Heinemann, 1985). The awards Morpurgo has received include: the 1995 Whitbread Children's Award for *Wreck of the Zanzibar* (Heinemann); the 1996 Nestlé Smarties Award for *The Butterfly Lion* (Collins) and the Red House Children's Book Award 2000 for *Kensuke's Kingdom* (Egmont). Titles shortlisted include *The Dancing Bear* (Collins,1992) – Writers' Guild Children's Book Award 1994 and the *Young Telegraph* Children's Paperback of the Year Award; *Wombat Goes Walkabout* (Collins) – the 1999 Whitbread Award and *Cool!* (Collins, 2002) – the *Blue Peter* Book Awards 2003. Other recent publications include *The Sleeping Sword* (Egmont, 2000); *Gentle Giant* (Collins, 2003) and *Private Peaceful* (Collins, 2003) which was also shortlisted for the Whitbread Award, 2003. In 1998, together with the late Ted Hughes, Morpurgo devised and set up the Children's Laureate to bring attention to the importance of children's writing, and to celebrate the quality of the best of children's publishing. In 1999 he was awarded an MBE for his services to youth and in May, 2003, he himself was appointed Children's Laureate – a post which is held for two years.

> 'We need to recognise the power of the storyteller, and how infectious that power can be, right the way across the range. There are a number of us in this country who can wave the flag and bang the drum. So, give me the drum.' *Publishing News*, January, 2004.

William Nicholson was born in 1948 and educated at Downside School near Bath. Having graduated in English literature from Christ's College, Cambridge in 1970, he joined the BBC as a documentary film maker. His TV play *Shadowlands* was later staged in the theatre, winning the *Evening Standard* Award in 1990 for best play and going on to win a Tony Award in the USA. He was later nominated for an Oscar for the screenplay. Nicholson has many film scripts to his credit and was nominated for a second Oscar for *Gladiator* as co-writer. His first children's book *The Wind Singer* (Egmont, 2000) won the Nestlé Smarties Gold Award (9–11 years) in 2000 and the *Blue Peter* Book of the Year Award in 2001. Its sequel *Slave of the Mastery* was published in 2001 and the final part of *The Wind on Fire* trilogy *Firesong* in 2002. His latest book *The Society of Others* was published by Doubleday (2004).

His advice to children who would like to become writers:

> 'Read a lot. Then start writing, and keep writing. Writers get better the more they write. Write about someone or something that excites you, or that you care about a lot. Don't give up. It may take a long time but be very determined. If one failure defeats you, you're not going to make it. Every failure should make you more determined – but more open to hearing the criticisms. It's hard I admit. You have to be a bit crazy. But it's also glorious.' Questionnaire on William Nicholson's website: www.williamnicholson.co.uk

Garth Nix was born in 1963 in Melbourne, Australia. Following a brief spell in a clerical post for the government, he gained a Bachelor of Arts in Professional Writing at the University of Canberra, graduating in 1986. Prior to this he had written numerous short stories, of which one was published in 1984. His first novel *The Ragwitch* was published in Australia in 1990, and in 1994 in the USA. Employment in the publishing industry followed before a spell as a marketing communications consultant. 1995 saw the publication of *Sabriel* (HarperCollins Australia) – the first in a trilogy of the same name. *Sabriel* won many awards in Australia, as well as in the USA, and in 2003 was nominated for Newcomer of the Year at the British Book Awards. The second and third books *Lirael* and *Abhorsen* in the fantasy series are published in the UK by HarperCollins. Collins is also the publisher for Nix's next series of seven books under the overall title *The Keys of the Kingdom*. The first of these, *Mister Monday*, was published in 2004, to be followed by *Grim Tuesday*. Nix has written another series of books for younger children entitled *The Seventh Tower*. He lives with his family in Sydney, near Coogee Beach.

His advice to aspiring writers:

'Read a lot, and read widely (not just in one genre or area). Write as often as you can, even if it's only a few paragraphs at a time. Submit a lot, even if you only get rejections (all writers get rejections). Most of all, don't give up.'

Christopher Paolini lives in Paradise Valley, Montana, USA. His parents are both published authors and as a child he read vast quantities of fantasy and science fiction. In 1998, aged fifteen, he left school and decided against further education as he wanted to write. By the beginning of 2002 he had finished the first book in his trilogy *Inheritance*, entitled *Eragon*, published by Knopf Books in 2003 – and by Doubleday in the UK in 2004. An instant bestseller in the USA and the UK, its film rights have already been bought by Fox 2000. Paolini is currently working on *Eldest*, the second book in the series.

'Write about what excites and moves you the most, otherwise your enthusiasm will never sustain you through an entire novel; be persistent and disciplined, otherwise someone more determined will take your place; and be humble enough to accept editorial criticism and learn all you can about your craft.'

Dav Pilkey was born in Cleveland, Ohio in 1966. From an early age he loved drawing cartoons and making people laugh, although this did not find favour with his teachers. While attending Kent State University one of his professors complimented him on his creative writing skills. Encouraged, he entered and won a competition for students who could write and illustrate their own books. *World War One* was published by Landmark Editions Inc the following year – the prize for the winner of the competition. In 1993 Pilkey moved to Oregon and continued developing the stories he had written and illustrated as a child. *The Adventures of Captain Underpants* was published by Scholastic in 1997. There are a further nine books in the series – the latest being *Captain Underpants and the Big, Bad Battle of the Bionic Booger Boy, Parts One and Two* (Scholastic, 2003). Orchard Books has published five of Pilkey's titles about a dragon, the first being *A Friend for Dragon* (1994). Using the name Sue Denim 'because it sounds like pseudonym' – he wrote four books in a series commencing with *Dumb Bunnies* (Scholastic, 1994). *Big Dog and Little Dog* (Harcourt, 1997) was the start of a series of five board books for toddlers. In 2000 Scholastic published *Ricky Ricotta's Mighty Robot* – the first of Pilkey's six books, illustrated by Martin Ontiveros, about a mouse. There are more than eleven other titles including *Dog Breath: The Horrible*

Trouble with Hally Tosis (Blue Sky Press, 1994) and *When Cats Dream* (Orchard Books, 1996).

Philip Pullman (www.philip-pullman.com) was born in Norwich in 1946. As both his father and stepfather were in the Royal Air Force, Pullman spent much of his childhood travelling and lived for a time in Australia and Zimbabwe. The family returned to live in North Wales when Pullman was aged eleven. A year after graduating from Exeter College, Oxford in 1968, he won the New English Library first novel competition. Thereafter he spent several years teaching before returning to lecture part-time at Westminster College, Oxford. His first children's novel *The Ruby in the Smoke*, the first of a quartet of Victorian thrillers, was published in 1985 by Oxford University Press. The other titles in the series are: *The Shadow in the North* (Random House Children's Publishers, 1988); *The Tiger in the Well* (Random House Children's Publishers, 1990) and *The Tin Princess* (Random House Children's Publishers, 1994). Author of over twenty books as well as a few plays and television scripts, Pullman is best known for his trilogy *His Dark Materials* which was adapted for The National Theatre in 2003. The first of the novels, *Northern Lights* (Scholastic, 1995), won the Carnegie Medal in the same year and was joint winner of the *Guardian* Fiction Prize in 1996. *The Subtle Knife* (Scholastic, 1997) was shortlisted for the Carnegie Medal, and *The Amber Spyglass* (Scholastic, 2000) won the British Book Awards Children's Book of the Year in 2000, as well as both the Whitbread Children's and Whitbread Book of the Year Awards in 2001. In the same year, he was also named Author of the Year by the British Book Awards. *Lyra's Oxford* (David Fickling Books, 2003) is the stepping stone between the trilogy and the next book. Other awards include the Nestlé Smarties Gold Award (9–11 years) for *The Firemaker's Daugher* (Corgi Juvenile, 1996) and the Nestlé Smarties Silver Award (1997) for *Clockwork: or All Wound Up*

(Corgi Juvenile, 1997). In 2002 Pullman was awarded the Eleanor Farjeon Prize for his contribution to children's writing, and in 2004 he received a CBE.

> 'As a passionate believer in the democracy of reading, I don't think it's the task of the author of a book to tell the reader what it means. The meaning of a story emerges in the meeting between the words on the page and the thoughts in the reader's mind.'

Louise Rennison was born in Leeds. When she was fifteen, she and her family moved to New Zealand but Louise was not happy there and, after six weeks, persuaded her parents to let her return to live with her grandparents in England. She admits her books are largely based on her own experiences as a teenager. Prior to writing teenage books, she wrote and performed a one-woman show *Stevie Wonder Felt My Face* which won acclaim both at the Edinburgh Festival and on tour, and went on to be televised by BBC2. She works regularly for Radio 4 and is a contributor to *Woman's Hour*. While writing a diary, *Dating Over 35*, for the *London Evening Standard*, she was invited by Piccadilly Press to write a book in the form of a teenage diary. *Angus, Thongs and Full-frontal Snogging: Confessions of Georgia Nicholson* was published by Piccadilly Press in 1999 and won the Nestlé Smarties Bronze Award (9–11 years) in the same year. This was followed by *It's OK, I'm Wearing Really Big Knickers* (Piccadilly Press, 2000); *On the Bright Side, I'm Now the Girlfriend of a Sex God* (HarperCollins, 2001) and *Knocked Out by My Nunga-Nungas* (Piccadilly Press, 2001), which was shortlisted for the 2002 Children's Book Award. Later titles include: *Dancing in My Nuddy Pants* (Piccadilly Press, 2002); *Away Laughing on a Fast Camel: Even More Confessions of Georgia Nicholson* (HarperCollins, 2004) and, *And That's When It Fell Off in My Hand* (HarperCollins, 2004).

Rennison now lives in Brighton. Her advice for young writers:

'Keep at it. Writing requires a sense of self and you need to have something that you really want to say. It is important to have a voice and you need to try that out. I also suggest that you get a good editor because when you are young there tends to be a fascination with self that needs paring down. After that, just have a bit of confidence. Also, charm never goes amiss!'

Michael Rosen was born in London in 1946. He started writing poetry when he was sixteen and had his first book, *Mind Your Own Business*, published by Scholastic in 1974. Both Rosen's parents were teachers, but he wanted to become an actor. However, he started training to be a doctor before changing to study English. Apart from his children's writing Rosen has written and presented several programmes for the BBC including Radio 4's *Treasure Islands* and *Word of Mouth*. He has worked with a variety of illustrators including Quentin Blake with whom he published: *Quick, Let's Get Out of Here* (Puffin, 1985), *Don't Put Mustard in the Custard* (Scholastic, 1985) and *Smelly Jelly, Smelly Fish* (Walker Books, 1986). In 1989, he won the Nestlé Smarties Gold Award for *We're Going on a Bear Hunt* (Walker Books), illustrated by Helen Oxenbury. Rosen has compiled numerous anthologies such as *The Kingfisher Book of Children's Poetry* (1985) and *The Kingfisher Book of Comic Verse* (1986). He was one of the first poets to visit schools and for his services to children's literature he received the Eleanor Farjeon Award in 1997. Most recent publications include: *Little Rabbit Foo Foo* (Walker Books, 2003); *Oww!* (Collins, 2003); *Snore!* (Collins 2004); *Howler* (Bloomsbury, 2004) and *Poems for the Very Young* (Kingfisher, 2004).

He says:

'Write about anything that matters to you, anything that intrigues you. Look for things that seem quirky or off the wall. Always be

willing to use the sounds of words and phrases and sentences that you hear around you. Everything that's in the air is there for us to use. Borrow it, break it up, move it around. It's there to play with.'
Young Writer

Tony Ross was born in London in 1938. After training at the Liverpool School of Art, he worked as a cartoonist, graphic designer and as an art director for an advertising agency, before becoming a senior lecturer in art at the Manchester Polytechnic. Now one of the best-known creators of original and traditional picture books, Ross has won numerous awards and his books are sold worldwide. His first title for Andersen Press – for whom he has now produced over sixty books – was *Goldilocks and the Three Bears* published in 1976. Best known are the series of books about a scruffy dog called Towser, written by Jeanne Willis, and the *Dr Xargle* series. *I Want My Potty* (1986) won the Dutch Silver Pencil Award for the best text by a foreign author in 1987. In 1986 *I'm Coming to Get You* (1984) won the German Children's Book Prize and in 1991 *Dr Xargle's Book of Earth Tiggers* was shortlisted and highly commended for the Kate Greenaway Medal. He has twice been shortlisted for the Nestlé Smarties Award – firstly in 1991 for *A Fairy Tale*, and secondly in 1994 for *The Second Princess*. With Jeanne Willis as author, he won the 2003 Smarties Silver Award (0–5 years) for *Tadpole's Promise*. Ross has illustrated works by numerous other authors including Roald Dahl, Michael Morpurgo and Michael Palin, and Francesca Simon's series of *Horrid Henry* books. Most recent titles for Andersen include: *I Don't Want to Go to Hospital* (2000); *I Want My Dummy!* (2001); *I Want a Sister* (2002); *I Want My Tooth* (2002); *I Don't Want to Go to Bed!* (2003) and *I Want My Mum!* (2004).

'Tony Ross is prolific and his zany imagination never seems to stall.'
The Observer

J. K. Rowling (jkrowling.com) was born in Chipping Sodbury in 1965. At the age of six, she wrote her first book *Rabbit*. Having gained a degree in French from Exeter University, she moved to London to work with Amnesty International. The idea for the series of seven *Harry Potter* books was conceived while on a delayed train journey from Manchester to London. Shortly afterwards she moved to Oporto in Portugal to teach English as a foreign language, and while there she met her first husband and became pregnant. However, the marriage did not last and she and her daughter returned to live in Edinburgh. A part-time teaching job followed by a bursary, awarded by the Scottish Arts Council, allowed her to finish her book. In 1997, after many rejections, Bloomsbury published *Harry Potter and the Philosopher's Stone*. It won the Nestlé Smarties Gold Medal (9–11 years), the British Book Awards Children's Book of the Year and the *Young Telegraph* Paperback of the Year, as well as two prestigious foreign awards – the Sorcières Prix in 1998 in France and the Premio Cento per la Letteratura Infantile 1998 in Italy. The second title *Harry Potter and the Chamber of Secrets* was published in 1998, again winning the Gold Smarties Award in 1998, the British Book Awards Children's Book of the Year 1998 and, additionally, the Scottish Arts Council Children's Book Award 1999. With the publication of *Harry Potter and the Prisoner of Azkaban* in 1999, Rowling won the Smarties Gold Medal for the third year running. It also won the Whitbread Children's Book of the Year, and she herself won the British Book Awards 1999 Author of the Year. *Harry Potter and the Goblet of Fire* (2000) had a first print run of one million copies and broke all records for the greatest number of books sold on the first day of publication. On this occasion she again won the Scottish Arts Council Book Award 2001, the Children's Book Award (9–11 years), plus the Hugo Award. In 2001 Rowling wrote two books in aid of Comic Relief: *Fantastic Beasts and Where to Find Them* and *Quidditch through the Ages*. The fifth title *Harry Potter and the* *val* (2002) and *The Slippery Slope* (2003). Three more are planned, and in 2002 *The Unauthorized Biography of Lemony Snicket* was also published by HarperCollins. Snicket is a bestseller in the UK as well as the USA, and in 2003 *The Ersatz Elevator* was shortlisted for the British Book Awards Children's Book of the Year. A film, based on the books, to be made by Paramount/Nickleodean Movies and starring Meryl Streep and Jude Law, is due for release in 2004. In an interview for Morrill Books, a San Francisco bookshop, Handler's advice to children who want to be writers was:

'Avoid wearing squeaky shoes when listening at keyholes.'

Jacqueline Wilson (www.kidsatrandomhouse.co.uk) was born in Bath, Somerset in 1945. When she was a year old, her parents moved to Kingston in Surrey. Wilson attended Coombe Girls' School in New Malden before embarking on a secretarial course. On seeing an advertisement seeking teenage writers, placed by the Dundee publisher D.C. Thompson, she decided to apply. She was offered the job and, aged seventeen, moved to Scotland. Thompson published *The Beano* and *The Dandy* and wanted to launch a magazine for teenagers. This was called *Jackie* and it is believed it may have been named after Wilson. In Dundee she met her future husband whom she married at the age of nineteen. They moved to London; he joined the police, and, aged twenty-one, Wilson gave birth to their daughter. Her first book to be accepted for publication was *Ricky's Birthday* (Macmillan), part of the *Nipper* series. At the beginning of her career she combined novel-writing with magazine stories. In 1987 *Glubbslyme* was published by Oxford University Press and it was republished by Corgi Juvenile in 1990. Her next book, *The Story of Tracy Beaker* (Doubleday, 1991), illustrated by Nick Sharratt, marked the beginning of her enormously successful career as a children's author. This title won the Sheffield Children's

Book Award in 1992 and was shortlisted for the 1991 Nestlé
Smarties Award, the Children's Book Award and the Carnegie
Medal. It has since been adapted for radio and is the basis of three
television serials and of a full-length film for the BBC. Since then all
Wilson's books have been illustrated by Nick Sharratt and published
by Doubleday in hardback, followed by a paperback edition produced by Corgi Juvenile.

She has either won, or been shortlisted for, every major children's
award in the UK. Her award-winning titles include: *The Bed and
Breakfast Star* (1994) – winner of the *Young Telegraph* Award 1995,
shortlisted for the Carnegie Medal and adapted for radio; *Double
Act* (1995) – overall winner Nestlé Smarties Award 1996 and also
winner category (9–11 years), overall winner Sheffield Children's
Book Award 1996 and winner of the shorter novel category, winner
of the Children's Book Award 1996, shortlisted for the Writers'
Guild Literary Award 1995 and for the *Young Telegraph* Award 1996
and adapted for the Polka Children's Theatre in 2000 and by herself
for Channel 4 in 2000; *Bad Girls* (1996) – winner of the Sheffield
Children's Award 1997 in the shorter novel category, shortlisted for
the Carnegie Medal 1997; *The Lottie Project* (1997) – winner of the
Stockport Children's Book Award 1998, highly commended for the
Sheffield Children's Book Award in the shorter novel category,
shortlisted for the Children's Book Award 1998 and adapted for the
Polka Theatre in 1999; *The Illustrated Mum* (1999) – British Book
Awards Children's Book of the Year 1999, winner of the *Guardian*
Children's Fiction Award 2000, highly commended for the Carnegie
Medal 1999, shortlisted for the Whitbread Children's Book Award
1999, shortlisted for the Children's Book Award 2000 and shortlisted
for the Sheffield Children's Book Award; *Lizzie Zipmouth* (1999) –
winner of the Nestlé Smarties Award (6–8 years) 2000 and of the
Children's Book Award 2001; and *Girls in Tears* (2002) – British Book
Awards Children's Book of the Year 2003. Recent titles include: *Lola*

Rose (2003); *Midnight* (2003) and *Best Friends* (2004). Wilson writes books for children of seven or eight, as well as a darker group of books, for older children, such as the *Girls in* . . . series. In a recent poll for the BBC *The Big Read*, four of Wilson's books were in the Top 100. She has sold over 15 million copies and been translated into more than twenty-three languages. For seventeen years Catherine Cookson was the most borrowed author from public libraries in the UK, but in 2004 the Public Lending Right announced that, for 2002–03, Jacqueline Wilson had taken the lead. For her services to literacy in schools she was awarded the OBE in 2002.

'Her appeal is extraordinary, and I think it's due to the fact that she writes directly – never down: she taps into something that young girls especially, but certainly boys too, recognise as being distinctively like themselves. She is very hard-working and very consistent; but the other interesting thing about her is that without moving away from her audience, she seems to be getting deeper and darker.' Philip Pullman, *The Guardian*

LISTINGS

UK Publishers with Children's Imprints

Andersen Press Ltd

20 Vauxhall Bridge Road, London SW1V 2SA

☎ 020 7840 8703/8700   Fax 020 7233 6263

Email andersenpress@randomhouse.co.uk

Website www.andersenpress.co.uk

Managing Director/Publisher *Klaus Flugge*
Editorial Director *Janice Thomson*
Editor, Fiction *Audrey Adams*

FOUNDED 1976 by Klaus Flugge and named after Hans Christian Andersen. Publishes children's high-quality picture books and fiction sold in association with Random House Children's Books. Seventy per cent of the books are sold as co-productions abroad. CHILDREN'S AUTHORS Ken Brown, Ruth Brown, Damon Burnard, Melvin Burgess, Lindsey Camp, Emma Chichester Clark, Gus Clarke, Roger Collinson, Patrick Cooper, Peta Coplans, Malachy Doyle, Robert Dodd, Philippe Dupasquier, Anne Fine, Michael Foreman, Nigel Gray, Paul Hess, Julia Jarman, Sarah Garland, Griselda Gifford, Tim Kennemore, Penny Kendall, Satoshi Kitamura, P. J. Lynch, David McKee, Colin McNaughton, Fiona Moodie, Sandy Nightingale, Hiawyn Oram, Chris Riddell, Mark Roberts, Tony Ross, Ralph Steadman, Paul Stewart, John Shelley, Hazel Townson, Chris Van Allsburg, Susan Varley, Max Velthuijs, Jeanne Willis. Unsolicited mss welcome for picture books;

LISTINGS

synopsis in the first instance for books for young readers up to age 12. No
poetry or short stories.

Anness Publishing Ltd
Hermes House, 88–89 Blackfriars Road, London SE1 8HA
☎ 020 7401 2077   Fax 020 7633 9499
Email info@anness.com
Website www.aquamarinebooks.com
Website www.lorenzbooks.com
Website www.southwaterbooks.com

Chairman/Managing Director *Paul Anness*
Publisher/Partner *Joanna Lorenz*

FOUNDED 1989. Publishes highly illustrated co-edition titles: general non-
fiction – cookery, crafts, interior design, gardening, photography, decorat-
ing, lifestyle and children's. IMPRINTS **Lorenz Books; Aquamarine; Hermes
House; Peony Press; Southwater**. CHILDREN'S AUTHORS David Alderton,
Petra Boase, Michael Bright, Jack Challoner, Michael Chinery, Marion Elliot,
John Farndon, Cecilia Fitzsimmons, Clare Gooden, Dr Jen Green, Michael
Harris, Peter Harrison, Dr John Haywood, Tom Jackson, Robin Kerrod,
Kate Lively, Fiona MacDonald, Tony Russell, Philip Steele, Barbara Taylor,
Ridney Walshaw.

Ashmolean Museum Publications
Ashmolean Museum, Beaumont Street, Oxford OX1 2PH
☎ 01865 278010   Fax 01865 278018
Email publications@ashmus.ox.ac.uk
Website www.ashmol.ox.ac.uk

Contact *Declan McCarthy*

The Ashmolean Museum, which is wholly owned by Oxford University,
was founded in 1683. The first publication appeared in 1890 but publishing
did not really start in earnest until the 1960s. Publishes European and
Oriental fine and applied arts, European archaeology and ancient history,

Egyptology and numismatics, for both adult and children's markets. No fiction, American/African art, ethnography, modern art or post-medieval history. Most publications are based on and illustrated from the Museum's collections. No unsolicited mss.

Atlantic Europe Publishing Co. Ltd

Greys Court Farm, Greys Court, Nr Henley on Thames RG9 4PG
☎ 01491 628188   Fax 01491 628189
Email writers@atlanticeurope.com
Website www.AtlanticEurope.com
Website www.curriculumVisions.com

Directors *Dr B.J. Knapp, D.L.R. McCrae*

Closely associated, since 1990, with Earthscape Editions packaging operation. Publishes full-colour, highly illustrated children's non-fiction in hardback for international co-editions and text books. Not interested in any other material. Main focus is on National Curriculum titles, especially in the fields of mathematics, science, technology, social history and geography. Unsolicited synopses and ideas for non-fiction curriculum-based books welcome by email only – does not accept material sent by post.

Autumn Publishing Ltd

Appledram Barns, Birdham Road, Chichester PO20 7EQ
☎ 01243 531660   Fax 01243 774433
Email autumn@autumnpublishing.co.uk
Website www.autumnpublishing.co.uk

Managing Director *Michael Herridge*
Editorial Director *Ingrid Goldsmid*

FOUNDED 1976, part of the Bonnier Group. Publishes baby and toddler books, children's activity, sticker and early learning books. No responsibility accepted for the return of unsolicited mss.

Award Publications Limited

1st Floor, 27 Longford Street, London NW1 3DZ

☎ 020 7388 7800   Fax 020 7388 7887

Email info@awardpublications.co.uk

FOUNDED 1958. Publishes children's books, both fiction and reference. IMPRINT **Horus Editions**. CHILDREN'S AUTHORS Jane Carruth, Jackie Andrews, Rene Cloke, Christine Pullein-Thompson, Josephine & Diana Pullein-Thompson, Lorna Hill, Jane Launchbury, Jean Chapman, Linda Jennings, Michael Bishop, Sue Hall, Val Biro, Hayden McAllister, Lesley Smith, Alan Fredman, Peter Adby. No unsolicited mss, synopses or ideas.

Barefoot Books Ltd

124 Walcot Street, Bath BA1 5BG

☎ 01225 322400   Fax 01225 322499

Email sales@barefootbooks.com

Website www.barefootbooks.com

Publisher *Tessa Strickland*
UK Editor *Natasha Carr*

FOUNDED in 1993. Publishes high-quality children's picture books, particularly new and traditional stories from a wide range of cultures. CHILDREN'S AUTHORS Polly Alakija, Naomi Adler, Roberta Arenson, Jules Bass, Tanya Batt, Clare Beaton, Jill Bennett, Laura Berkeley, Stella Blackstone, Sarah Jane Boss, Philippa-Alys Browne, Quint Buchholz, Juliet Sharman Burke, Lucy Byng, Catherine Chambers, Faustin Charles, Sherab Chodzin, Karen Christensen, Wendy Cooling, Gael Cresp, Joanna Crosse, Sabrina Dearborn, Malachy Doyle, Jim Edmiston, Josephine Evetts-Secker, Mary Finch, Evelyn Foster, Mordicai Gerstein, Cherry Gilchrist, Laurel Dee Gugler, Felicity Hansen, Robin Harris, Rebecca Hazell, Mary Hoffman, Sandra Ann Horn, Rod Hull, Shahrukh Husain, Alexandra Kohn, Laurie Krebs, Mary Lister, Hugh Lupton, Raouf Mama, Beatrice Masini, Caitlin Matthews, John Matthews, Paula Metcalf, Willemien Min, Caroline Mockford, Burleigh Mutén, Judith Nicholls, Joanne Oppenheim, Paul Lewis Owen, Papa Oyibo, Fran

Parnell, Andrew Fusek Peters, James Riordan, Sheena Roberts, Lillian Hammer Ross, Susan L. Roth, Patrick Ryan, Nikki Siegen-Smith, Sylvia Sikundar, Rina Singh, Wolfgang Somary, Barbara Soros, Laya Steinberg, Tessa Strickland, Susan Summers, Edith Tarbescu, Wafa Tarnowska, Alice Taylor, Aleksei Tolstoy, David Tse, Jatinder Verma, Marleen Vermeulen, Guido Visconti, Richard Walker, Eliabeth Stuart Warfel, Fiona Waters, Laura Whipple, Amanda White, Susan Whitfield, Rose Williams, Margaret Olivia Wolfson, Jakki Wood. No unsolicited mss; see website for submission guidelines.

Barny Books

Hough on the Hill, Near Grantham NG32 2BB
☎ 01400 250246/01522 790009   Fax 01400 251737

Managing Director/Editorial Head *Molly Burkett*
Business Manager *Tom Cann*
Approx. Annual Turnover £10,000

FOUNDED with the aim of encouraging new writers and illustrators. Publishes mainly children's books but also adult fiction and non-fiction. Offers schools' projects where students help to produce books. CHILDREN'S AUTHORS Caspian Ashworth, Molly Burkett, Liz Caldicott, Nicola Davies, N. J. Dinsdale, Sheralee Iglehart, Robert Montgomery, Lesley Moran, Jenny Webb, Keith West. Too small a concern to have the staff/resources to deal with unsolicited mss. Writers with strong ideas should approach Molly Burkett by letter in the first instance. Also runs a readership and advisory service for new writers (£10 fee for short stories or illustrations; £25 fee for full-length stories).

Barrington Stoke

Sandeman House, Trunk's Close, 55 High Street, Edinburgh EH1 1SR
☎ 0131 557 2020   Fax 0131 557 6060
Email info@barringtonstoke .co.uk
Website www.barringtonstoke.co.uk

Chairman *David Croom*
Managing Director *Sonia Raphael*
Editorial Head *Anna Gibbons*
Approx. Annual Turnover £400,000

FOUNDED in 1998 to publish books for 'reluctant, disenchanted and under-confident' young readers. Produces a series of audio books and issues teachers' notes to acccompany teenage fiction titles. DIVISIONS **4u2read.OK** for children aged 8–13 with a reading age below 8; **Fiction** for 8–13-year olds. TITLES *Living With Vampires; Tod in Biker City.* **Teenage Fiction** TITLES *Runaway Teacher; No Stone Unturned.* CHILDREN'S AUTHORS Rachel Anderson, Philip Ardagh, Bernard Ashley, David Belbin, Julie Bertagna, Malorie Blackman, Tony Bradman, Theresa Breslin, Eric Brown, Melvin Burgess, Peter Clover, Yvonne Coppard, Peter Crowther, Annie Dalton, Isla Dewar, Colin Dowland, Terry Dreary, Alan Durant, Vivian French, Adèle Geras, Alan Gibbons, Pippa Goodheart, Keith Gray, Ann Halam, Diana Hendry, Douglas Hill, Nigel Hinton, Mary Hoffman, Mary Hooper, Lesley Howarth, Pete Johnson, Ann Jungman, Brian Keaney, Michael Lawrence, James Lovegrove, Catherine MacPhail, Wes Magee, Lynne Markham, Anthony Masters, Jonathan Meres, Michaela Morgan, Michael Morpurgo, Mark Morris, Jenny Oldfield, Judith O'Neill, Alison Prince, Bali Rai, Shoo Rayner, Rosie Rushton, Sara Sheridan, Dee Shulman, Norman Silver, Jeremy Strong, Hazel Townson, Kaye Umansky. Books commissioned via literary agents only. *No* unsolicited material.

BBC Books

BBC Worldwide Ltd , 80 Wood Lane, London W12 0TT
☎ 020 8433 2000   Fax 020 8433 3707
Website www.bbcworldwide.com

Publishing Director *Robin Wood*

Publishes TV tie-in and some stand-alone titles, including books which, though linked with BBC television or radio, may not simply be the 'book of the series'. Also TV tie-in titles for children. Unsolicited mss (which come in at the rate of about 40 weekly) are rarely accepted. However, strong ideas well expressed will always be considered, and promising letters stand a chance of further scrutiny.

A.&C. Black Publishers Ltd

Alderman House, 37 Soho Square, London W1D 3QZ
☎ 020 7758 0200   Fax 020 7758 0222
Email enquiries@acblack.com
Website www.acblack.com

Chairman *Nigel Newton*
Managing Director *Jill Coleman*
Publishing Director, Reference *Jonathan Glasspool*
Approx. Annual Turnover £10.5 million

Publishes children's and educational books, including music, for 3–15-year-olds, arts and crafts, ceramics, fishing, ornithology, nautical, reference, sport, theatre and travel. Bought by **Bloomsbury Publishing** in May 2000. Owns *Whitaker's Almanack* and children's publisher **Andrew Brodie Publications**. IMPRINTS **Adlard Coles Nautical**; **Christopher Helm**; **The Herbert Press**; **Pica Press**. TITLES *New Mermaid* drama series; *Who's Who*; *Writers' & Artists' Yearbook*; *Know the Game* sports series; *Blue Guides* travel series; *Rockets* and *Black Cats* children's series. CHILDREN'S AUTHORS Scoular Anderson, Linda Bailey, David Belbin, Melvin Burgess, Terry Deary, Michael Hardcastle, Rose Impey, Ann Jungman, Anthony Masters, Maggie Pearson, Sallie Purkiss, Frank Rogers, Dee Shulman, Peter Utton, Karen Wallace, Colin West, Philip Wooderson. Initial enquiry appreciated before submission of mss.

Bloomsbury Publishing Plc

38 Soho Square, London W1D 3HB
☎ 020 7494 2111   Fax 020 7434 0151
Website www.bloomsburymagazine.com

Chairman/Chief Executive *Nigel Newton*
Publishing Directors *Alexandra Pringle, Liz Calder, Kathy Rooney, Sarah Odedina, Arzu Tahsin*
Approx. Annual Turnover £61 million+

FOUNDED in 1986 by Nigel Newton, David Reynolds, Alan Wherry and Liz Calder. Over the following years Bloomsbury titles were to appear regularly on *The Sunday Times* bestseller list and many of its authors have gone on to win prestigious literary prizes. In 1991 Nadine Gordimer won the **Nobel Prize for Literature**; Michael Ondaatje's *The English Patient* won the 1992 **Booker Prize**; in 1997 Anne Michaels' *Fugitive Pieces* won both the **Orange Prize for Fiction** and the Guardian Fiction Prize. J.K. Rowling's *Harry Potter and the Philosopher's Stone, Harry Potter and the Chamber of Secrets* and *Harry Potter and the Prisoner of Azkaban* won the **Nestlé Smarties Book Prize** in 1997, 1998 and 1999 respectively. Margaret Atwood's *The Blind Assassin* won the **Booker Prize** in 2000. Published *The Encarta World English Dictionary* in 1999. Started Bloomsbury USA in 1998. Acquired **A.&C. Black Publishers Ltd** in May 2000, **Peter Collin Publishing Ltd** in September 2002 and Berlin Verlag in 2003. Publishes literary fiction and non-fiction, including general reference; also audiobooks. CHILDREN'S AUTHORS Giles Andreae, Laurence Anholt, Dawn Apperley, Quentin Blake, Tony Bradman, Herbie Brennan, Angela Carter, Lynne Chapman, Gennifer Choldenko, Sharon Creech, Malachy Doyle, Debi Gliori, Pippa Goodhart, Mary Hoffman, Mary Hooper, Nichola McAuliffe, Roger McGough, Marjorie Newman, Chloë Rayban, Celia Rees, Shen Roddie, Michael Rosen, J. K. Rowling, Louis Sachar, Lane Smith, William Steig, Jeanette Winterson, Benjamin Zephaniah. Unsolicited mss and synopses for adult titles only; no poetry.

The Book Guild Ltd

Temple House, 25 High Street, Lewes BN7 2LU
☎ 01273 472534   Fax 01273 476472
Email info@bookguild.co.uk
Website www.bookguild.co.uk

Chairman *George M. Nissen, CBE*
Managing Director *Carol Biss*

FOUNDED 1982. Publishes fiction, human interest, media, children's fiction, academic, natural history, naval and military, biography, art. Expanding mainstream list plus developing the human interest/media genre.

DIVISIONS **Human Interest; Biography; Fiction; Mind, Body, Spirit; Children's Fiction** CHILDREN'S AUTHORS V. Alsoton, C. Ashworth, J. Berryman, D. Bond, L. Bower, M. Brown, Robin Cousins, C. Coyne, Richard Davids, Maureen Fry, Cathrine Garnell, M. Gava, L. Heighes, L. Kilburn, S. Kirk, Susanne Lakin, Rosemary Linnell, A. Mac, Sue Mackay, A. McRoberts, C. Mellor, A. Merhege, Geoffrey Palmer and Nick Lloyd, G. Partridge, Ida Pearson, Christine Perkins, R. Pilkington, J. Priestly, B. Russell, M. Scott, A. Taylor, A. and W. Turner, S. Varley. Unsolicited mss, ideas and synopses welcome.

The British Museum Press

46 Bloomsbury Street, London WC1B 3QQ
☎ 020 7323 1234   Fax 020 7436 7315
Website www.britishmuseum.co.uk

Managing Director *Andrew Thatcher*
Director of Publishing *Alasdair Macleod*

The book publishing division of The British Museum Company Ltd. FOUNDED 1973 as British Museum Publications Ltd; relaunched 1991 as British Museum Press. Publishes ancient history, archaeology, ethnography, art history, exhibition catalogues, guides, children's books, and all official publications of the British Museum. CHILDREN'S AUTHORS Penny Bateman, Diana Bentley, Steve and Megumi Biddle, Susan Bird, Jenny Chattlington, Janet Coles, Roscoe Cooper, Mike Corbishley, Carolyn Croll, Stephen Crummy, Carol Donoughue, Jim Farrant, Joyce Filer, Neil Grant, John Green, Rayna Green, Patricia Hansom, Pam Harper, Geraldine Harris, John Harris, George Hart, Carolyn Howitt, Ralph Jackson, Simon James, Ian Leins, Judy Lindsay, Lise Manniche, Angela McDonald, Neil Morris, Emma Myers, John Orna-Ornstein, Richard Parkinson, Delia Pemberton, James Putnam, Sandy Ransford, Hans Rashbrook, John Reeve, Catherine Roehrig, Sean Sheehan, Neal Spencer, John Taylor, Claire Thorne, Clio Whittaker, David M. Wilson, Katharine Wiltshire, Richard Woff, Catherine Wood. Synopses and ideas for books welcome.

Caxton Publishing Group

20 Bloomsbury Street, London WC1B 3JH

☎ 020 7636 7171   Fax 020 7636 1922

Email office@caxtonpublishing.com

Website www.caxtonpublishing.com

Chairman *Stephen Hill*
Managing Director *John Maxwell*
Approx. Annual Turnover £4 million

FOUNDED 1999. Specialises in reprinting out-of-print works for the 'value' market worldwide and commissioning new general non-fiction publications in reference, cookery, gardening and children's. DIVISIONS/IMPRINTS **Brock-hampton Press Ltd** Children's fiction and non-fiction. **Caxton Editions Ltd** General non-fiction, reference and military. **Knight Paperbacks Ltd** Fiction. CHILDREN'S AUTHORS Anne Christie, Hilary Hammond, Mandy Hancock, Jane Pilgrim. No unsolicited mss; synopses and ideas welcome; send letter in the first instance.

Chicken House Publishing

2 Palmer Street, Frome BA11 1DS

☎ 01373 454488   Fax 01373 454499

Email chickenhouse@doublecluck.com

Chairman/Managing Director *Barry Cunningham*

Children's publishing house founded in 2000. Publishes books 'that are aimed at real children' – fiction, original picture books, gift books and fun non-fiction. CHILDREN'S AUTHORS Melvin Burgess, Kevin Brooks, Caroline Jayne Church, Sarah Delmege, Chitra Banerjee Divakaruni, Teresa Doran, Heather Dyer, Jamieson Findlay, Cornelia Funke, Pippa Goodhart, Cathy Hopkins, Charlotte Houston, Elizabeth Kay, Paeony Lewis, Erik L'Homme, James Mayhew, Michael Molloy, Pam Munoz, Liz & Kate Pope, Katherine Roberts, Mark Sperring, Ruth Louise Symes, Vineeta Vijayaraghavan. 'We are always on the lookout for new talent.' Unsolicited material welcome; send letter with synopsis and sample chapters.

Child's Play (International) Ltd

Ashworth Road, Bridgemead, Swindon SN5 7YD

☎ 01793 616286   Fax 01793 512795

Email allday@childs-play.com

Website www.childs-play.com

Chief Executive *Neil Burden*

FOUNDED in 1972, Child's Play is an independent publisher specialising in learning through play, whole child development, life-skills and values. Publishes books, games and A-V materials. CHILDREN'S AUTHORS Pam Adams, Sue Baker, Michael Evans, Tina Freeman, Andrew Fusek Peters, Toni Goffer, Richard Hatfield, Penny Ives, Annie Kubler, Arthur John L'Hommedieu, Kees Moerbeek, Amanda Montgomery-Higham, Gervaise Phinn, Mandy Ross, Jess Stockham. Unsolicited mss welcome. Send s.a.e. for return or response. Expect to wait two months for a reply.

Christian Focus Publications

Geanies House, Fearn, Tain IV20 1TW

☎ 01862 871011   Fax 01862 871699

Email info@christianfocus.com

Website www.christianfocus.com

Chairman *R.W.M. Mackenzie*
Managing Director *William Mackenzie*
Editorial Manager *Willie Mackenzie*
Children's Editor *Catherine Mackenzie*

FOUNDED 1979 to produce children's books for the co-edition market. Now a major producer of Christian books. Publishes adult and children's books, including some fiction for children but not adults. No poetry. Publishes for all English-speaking markets, as well as the UK. IMPRINTS **Christian Focus** General books; **Mentor** Study books; **Christian Heritage** Classic reprints. CHILDREN'S AUTHORS Dick Anderson, Horace Banner, Joel R. Deeke, Anne de Vries, Sinclair Ferguson, Nancy Gorrell, Sheila Jacobs, Diana Kleyn, Sarah Knights Johnson, Carine Mackenzie, F. L. Mortimer, Ross Woodman.

Unsolicited mss, synopses and ideas welcome from Christian writers. See website for submission criteria.

Chrysalis Children's Books

The Chrysalis Building, Bramley Road, London W10 6SP
☎ 020 7314 1400   Fax 020 7314 1598
Email firstinitialsurname@chrysalisbooks.co.uk
Website www.chrysalisbooks.com

Publisher *Sarah Fabiny*

Part of the **Chrysalis Books Group**. Publishes all kinds of children's books from fun books to illustrated classics and educational books under the following DIVISIONS: **Education** Editorial Manager *Joyce Bentley*. Publishes children's non-fiction in all curriculum areas. TITLES *Start Writing; Art for All; Speaking and Listening; Art Revolutions; Strange Histories; Talking About.* No unsolicited mss. Synopses and ideas for books welcome from experienced children's writers. **Pre-School and Fiction** Editorial Manager *Liz Flanagan*. Publishes children's picture, novelty and gift books for ages 0–10. TITLES *War Boy; The Story of the Litle Mole Who Knew It Was None of His Business; Elephant Elements; Fairy Tales and Fantastic Stories.* No unsolicited mss. **Trade Non-Fiction** Editorial Head *Honor Head*. Publishes innovative and interactive children's books including novelty books, popular non-fiction, licensed characters. CHILDREN'S AUTHORS R. Tucker Abbott, Kate Banks, Jean-Luc Barbauneau, Kate Barnham, Paul Bennett, Dr Michael Benton, Susie Brooks, Moira Butterfield, Jannell Cannon, Francesca Chessa, Anna Claybourne, John Cooper, Alan Coren, Pie Corbett, Lyn Coutts, Andrew Crowson, Anna Currey, Jon Day, Janet de Saulles, Andy Dixon, Gordon Dryden, Michael Foreman, Pam Forey, Lynne Gibbs, Jen Green, Nicholas Harris, Troon Harrison, M.A. Harvey, Heinrich Hoffman, Werner Holzwarth, Michael Irwin, Leslie Jackman, David Jefferis, Terry Jones, Geoffrey Kibby, Robin Lawrie, Gerald Legg, Edwina Lewis, Sylvia Llaguno, Claire Llewellyn, Fiona MacDonald, Chris Maynard, George C. McGavin, Jacqueline McQuade, Alan Mitchell, Nicola Moon, Rowland Morgan, Sally Morgan, Michael Morpurgo, Neil Morris, Nanette Newman, Chris Oxlade,

Graham Percy, Fran Pickering, Nik Pollard, Sandy Ransford, Peter Riley, Jackie Robb, Thelma Robb, David Roberts, Lynn Roberts, Shen Roddie, Anne Rooney, Colin Rose, Angela Royston, Manja Stojic, Bernie Stringle, Lucy Su, Bill Thompson, Sian Tucker, Nick Ward, Ken Wilson-Max, Nicola Wright, Jay Young. No unsolicited mss.

Compendium Publishing Ltd

43 Frith Street, London W1D 4SA
☎ 020 7287 4570   Fax 020 7494 0583
Email compendiumpub@aol.com

Managing Director *Alan Greene*
Editorial Director *Simon Forty*

FOUNDED 1996. Publishes and packages for international publishing companies – general non-fiction: history, reference, hobbies, children's and educational transport and militaria. No unsolicited mss; synopses and ideas preferred.

Constable & Robinson Ltd

3 The Lanchesters, 162 Fulham Palace Road, London W6 9ER
☎ 020 8741 3663   Fax 020 8748 7562
Email enquiries@constablerobinson.com
Website www.constablerobinson.com

Non-Executive Chairman *Benjamin Glazebrook*
Managing Director *Nick Robinson*
Directors *Jan Chamier, Nova Jayne Heath, Adrian Andrews*

Constable & Co FOUNDED in 1890 by Archibald Constable, a grandson of Walter Scott's publisher. Robinson Publishing Ltd founded in 1983 by Nick Robinson. In December 1999 Constable and Robinson combined their individual shareholdings into a single company, Constable & Robinson Ltd. IMPRINTS **Constable** (Hardbacks) Editorial Director *Carol O'Brien* Publishes biography and autobiography, crime fiction, general and military history, psychology, travel, climbing, landscape photography and outdoor pursuits guidebooks. **Robinson** (Paperbacks) Senior Commissioning Editor *Krystyna Green* Publishes crime, science fiction, *Daily Telegraph* health books, the Mammoth series, psychology, true crime, military history and *Smarties* children's books. CHILDREN'S AUTHORS Mike Ashley, Jasmine Birtles, Paul Eldin, Anita Ganeri, Hugh Jears, David & Liza Mostyn, Michael Powell, Sandy Ransford, Deri Robins, Richard Robinson, Justin Scroggie. Unsolicited sample chapters, synopses and ideas for books welcome. No mss; no email submissions. Enclose return postage.

Dorling Kindersley Ltd

Part of the Penguin Group, 80 Strand, London WC2R ORL

☎ 020 7010 3000   Fax 020 7010 6060

Website www.dk.com

Chief Executive *Anthony Forbes Watson*
Managing Director *Andrew Welham*
Publisher *Christopher Davis*

FOUNDED 1974. Packager and publisher of illustrated non-fiction: cookery, crafts, gardening, health, travel guides, atlases, natural history and children's information and fiction. Launched a US imprint in 1991 and an Australian imprint in 1997. Acquired Henderson Publishing in 1995 and was purchased by Pearson plc for £311 million in 2000. DIVISIONS Adult: **Travel/Reference** Publisher *Douglas Amrine*; **General/Lifestyle** Publisher *John Roberts*. Children's: **Reference** Publisher *Miriam Farby*; **PreSchool/ Primary** Publisher *Sophie Mitchell*. IMPRINTS **Ladybird; Ladybird Audio; Funfax; Eyewitness Guides; Eyewitness Travel Guides.** CHILDREN'S AUTHORS Peter Ackroyd, Russell Ash, Stephen Biesty, Jane Bull, Heather Coupar, David Eckold, Debbie Gliori, Steve Levine, David Macaulay, Steve Noon, Nellie Shepherd, Carol Voderman, Dr Robert Winston. Unsolicited synopses/ideas for books welcome.

Dref Wen

28 Church Road, Whitchurch CF14 2EA

☎ 029 2061 7860 Fax 029 2061 0507

Email gwilym@drefwen.com

Chairman *R. Boore*
Managing Director *G. Boore*

FOUNDED 1970. Publishes Welsh language and bilingual children's books, Welsh and English educational books for Welsh learners. CHILDREN'S AUTHORS Bob Eynon, Nicholas Daniels, Gwyn Morgan, Martin Morgan.

Egmont Books Limited

239 Kensington High Street, London W8 6SA

☎ 020 7761 3500 Fax 020 7761 3510

Email firstname.lastname@ecb.egmont.com

Website www.egmont.co.uk

Managing Director *Fiona Clarke*
Publishing Director *David Riley*
Fiction & Picture Books *Cally Poplak*

Part of the Egmont Group (Copenhagen), Egmont Books publishes children's picture books, fiction, non-fiction, licensed characters, baby and toddler books and home learning. CHILDREN'S AUTHORS Malorie Blackman, Tony Bradman, Theresa Breslin, Jeff Brown, Ann Bryant, Kevin Crossley-Holland, Julia Donaldson, Malachy Doyle, Dorothy Edwards, Franzeska G. Ewart, Jan Fearnley, Anne Fine, Jamila Gavin, Pippa Goodhart, Colin Hawkins, Rose Impey, Dick King-Smith, Penelope Lively, Michelle Mogorian, Marilyn McLaughlin, Lydia Monks, Bel Mooney, Michael Morpurgo, Mary Murphy, William Nicholson, Jenny Nimmo, Caroline Pitcher, Dodi Smith, Lemony Snicket, Robert Swindells, Robert Westall, Jacqueline Wilson, Selina Young. Synopses and sample chapters welcome; approach in writing with s.a.e. marked for the attention of 'The Reader'. 'We regret that we are unable to return unsolicited material without s.a.e.'

Emma Treehouse Ltd

2nd Floor, The Old Brewhouse, Lower Charlton Trading Estate,
Shepton Mallet BA4 5QE
☎ 01749 330529   Fax 01749 330544
Email richard.powell4@virgin.net
Website www.emmatreehouse.com

Co-Directors *Richard Powell, David Bailey*
Approx. Annual Turnover £1 million

FOUNDED 1992. Publishes children's pre-school novelty books. No mss.
Illustrations, synopses and ideas for books welcome; write in the first
instance.

Evans Brothers Ltd

2A Portman Mansions, Chiltern Street, London W1U 6NR
☎ 020 7487 0920   Fax 020 7487 0921
Email sales@evansbrothers.co.uk
Website www.evansbooks.co.uk

Managing Director *Stephen Pawley*
International Publishing Director *Brian Jones*
UK Publisher *Su Swallow*
Approx. Annual Turnover £4.5 million

FOUNDED 1908 by Robert and Edward Evans. Originally published educational journals, books for primary schools and teacher education. After
rapid expansion into popular fiction and drama, both were sacrificed to a
major programme of educational books for schools in East and West Africa.
A UK programme was launched in 1986 followed by the acquisition of
Hamish Hamilton's non-fiction list for children in 1990. Acquired interests
in Cherrytree Books and Zero to Ten in 1999. Publishes UK children's and
educational books, and educational books for Africa, the Caribbean and
Latin America. IMPRINTS **Cherrytree Books**; **Zero to Ten** trade under Zero
to Ten Ltd at the Evans address above. CHILDREN'S AUTHORS Janine Amos,
Jill Atkins, Hilary Burningham, Meg Clibbon, Patrick Cummings, Kathy

Elgin, Pauline Francis, Vivian French, Anita Ganeri, Christine Hatt, Robin Lawrie, John Malam, Anna Nilsen, David Orme, Jillian Powell, Chris Powling, Hilary Robinson, Stewart Ross, Sue Vyner, Fiona Waters, Keith West, Brian Williams. Unsolicited mss, synopses and ideas for books welcome.

Everyman's Library
Northburgh House, 10 Northburgh Street, London EC1V 0AT
☎ 020 7566 6350   Fax 020 7490 3708
Email katy@everyman.uk.com

Publisher *David Campbell*
Approx. Annual Turnover £3.5 million

ESTABLISHED 1906. Publishes hardback classics of world literature, pocket poetry anthologies, children's books and travel guides. Publishes no new titles apart from poetry anthologies; only classics (no new authors). AUTHORS include Bulgakov, Bellow, Borges, Heller, Marquez, Nabokov, Naipaul, Orwell, Rushdie, Updike, Waugh and Wodehouse. No unsolicited mss.

Faber & Faber Ltd
3 Queen Square, London WC1N 3AU
☎ 020 7465 0045   Fax 020 7465 0034
Website www.faber.co.uk

Chief Executive *Stephen Page*
Approx. Annual Turnover £13 million

Geoffrey Faber founded the company in the 1920s, with T.S. Eliot as an early recruit to the board. The original list was based on contemporary poetry and plays (the distinguished backlist includes Eliot, Auden and MacNeice). Publishes poetry and drama, children's, fiction, film, music, politics, biography. DIVISIONS **Fiction** Editor-in-Chief *Jon Riley*; **Children's** *Suzy Jenvey, Julia Wells*; **Film** *Walter Donohue*; **Plays** *Dinah Wood*; **Music** *Belinda Matthews*; **Poetry** *Paul Keegan*; **Non-fiction** *Neil Belton, Julian Loose*.

CHILDREN'S AUTHORS Philip Ardagh, Anne Bailey, Helen Cresswell, Terry Deary, Malachy Doyle, Carol Ann Duffy, Ricky Gervais, Michael Hardcastle, Shirley Hughes, Garrison Keillor, Gene Kemp, Michael Morpurgo, Susan Price, Russell Stannard, G.P. Taylor.

Floris Books

15 Harrison Gardens, Edinburgh EH11 1SH

☎ 0131 337 2372   Fax 0131 347 9919

Email floris@florisbooks.co.uk

Website www.florisbooks.co.uk

Managing Director *Christian Maclean*
Editors *Christopher Moore, Gale Winskill*
Approx. Annual Turnover £350,000

FOUNDED 1977. Publishes books related to the Steiner movement, including The Christian Community, as well as arts & crafts, children's (including fiction with a Scottish theme), history, religious, science, social questions and Celtic studies. CHILDREN'S AUTHORS Gill Arbuthnott, Theresa Breslin, Maureen Dahlberg, Shelley Davidow, Lavinia Derwent, Daniela Drescher, Irene Watts. No unsolicited mss. Synopses and ideas for books welcome.

Geddes & Grosset

David Dale House, New Lanark ML11 9DJ

☎ 01555 665000   Fax 01555 665694

Publishers *Ron Grosset, R. Michael Miller*
Approx. Annual Turnover £3 million

FOUNDED 1989. Publisher of children's and reference books. Unsolicited mss, synopses and ideas welcome. No adult fiction.

Gomer

Llandysul SA44 4JL

☎ 01559 362371   Fax 01559 363758

Email gwasg@gomer.co.uk
Website www.gomer.co.uk

Chairman/Managing Director *J.E. Lewis*

FOUNDED 1892. Publishes adult fiction and non-fiction, children's fiction and educational material in English and Welsh. IMPRINTS **Gomer** *Bethan Mair, Bruan James* (Welsh editors), *Ceri Wyn Jones* (English). **Pont Books** *Sioned Lleinau, Helen Evans, Morys Rhys, Mairwen Prys Jones* (Welsh children's editors). CHILDREN'S AUTHORS Suzanne Carpenter, Phil Carradice, Clare Cooper, Nicola Davies, Malachy Doyle, Catherine Fisher, Rex Harley, Catherine Johnson, Jac Jones, Sian Lewis, Mary Medlicott, Ruth Morgan, Mary Oldham, Julie Rainsbury, Jenny Sullivan. No unsolicited mss, synopses or ideas. No English books for children.

Graham-Cameron Publishing & Illustration

The Studio, 23 Holt Road, Sheringham NR26 8NB
☎ 01263 821333   Fax 01263 821334
Email firstname@graham-cameron-illustration.com
Also at: 59 Redvers Road, Brighton, East Sussex BN2 4BF
☎ 01273 385890

Editorial Director *Mike Graham-Cameron*
Art Director *Helen Graham-Cameron*
Marketing Director *Duncan Graham-Cameron* (at Brighton address)

FOUNDED 1984 as a packaging operation. Publishes illustrated books for children and adults for institutions and business. Has 37 contracted book illustrators concentrating on educational and children's books. *Absolutely no* unsolicited mss.

HarperCollins Publishers Ltd

77–85 Fulham Palace Road, London w6 8JB
☎ 020 8741 7070   Fax 020 8307 4440
Website www.harpercollins.co.uk

Also at: Westerhill Road, Bishopbriggs, Glasgow G64 2QT
☎ 0141 772 3200   Fax 0141 306 3119

CEO/Publisher *Victoria Barnsley*

HarperCollins is one of the top three book publishers in the UK, with a wider range of books than any other publisher; from cutting-edge contemporary fiction to block-busting thrillers, from fantasy literature and children's stories to enduring classics. The wholly-owned division of News Corporation also publishes a wide selection of non-fiction including history, celebrity memoirs, biography, popular science, mind, body and spirit, dictionaries, maps and reference books. HarperCollins is also the third largest education publisher in the UK.

GENERAL BOOKS DIVISION Managing Director *Amanda Ridout*
Harper Fiction Publisher *Lynne Drew*. IMPRINTS **HarperCollins**; **Collins Crime**; **Voyager**. **Harper Press** Managing Director/Publisher *Caroline Michel*. IMPRINTS **Fourth Estate**; **HarperCollins Non-Fiction** Publishing Director *Michael Fishwick*; **HarperPerennial** Publisher *Venetia Butterfield*.
HarperCollins Children's Division Managing Director *Sally Gritten*; Publishing Directors *Gillie Russell* (Fiction),*Venetia Davie* (Properties), *Sue Buswell* (Picture Books) Quality picture books and book and tape sets for under-7s; fiction for age 6 up to young adult. IMPRINTS **Lions**; **Collins Picture Books**; **Collins Jet**; **Collins Teacher**. CHILDREN'S AUTHORS Jez Alborough, Berlie Doherty, Michael Bond, Nick Butterworth, Emma Chichester Clarke, Annie Dalton, Jan Fearnley, Vivian French, Maeve Friel, Mark Haddon, Colin & Jacqui Hawkins, Rose Impey, Robin Jarvis, Diana Wynne Jones, Ann Jungman, Fiona MacDonald, Geraldine McCaughrean, Michael Morpurgo, Beverly Naidoo, Nanette Newman, Jenny Nimmo, Garth Nix, Darren Shan, Brian Paterson, Louise Rennison, Katherine Roberts, Michael Rosen, Tony Ross, Jean Ure, Ian Whybrow.
HARPERENTERTAINMENT Managing Director/Publisher *Trevor Dolby* **Collins Willow**; **HarperCollins Audio**; **Estates** IMPRINT **Tolkien**.
Thorsons/Element Managing Director *Belinda Budge*.

COLLINS
Managing Director *Thomas Webster*
Collins Reference Division Publishing Director *Sarah Bailey* IMPRINTS
Collins; Collins Gem; New Naturalist Library; Times Books; Jane's.
Collins/Times Maps and Atlases. Collins Dictionaries/COBUILD.
Collins Education Division Managing Director *Jim Green* Books, CD-ROMs
and online material for UK schools and colleges.

Hodder Headline Ltd

338 Euston Road, London NW1 3BH
☎ 020 7873 6000   Fax 020 7873 6024
Website www.hodderheadline.co.uk

Group Chief Executive *Tim Hely Hutchinson*
Approx. Annual Turnover £130 million

Formed in June 1993 through the merger of Headline Book Publishing and
Hodder & Stoughton. Headline was formed in 1986 and had grown
dramatically, whereas Hodder & Stoughton was 125 years old with a
diverse range of publishing. The company was acquired by WHSmith plc
in 1999. Purchased **John Murray (Publishers) Ltd** in 2002.
DIVISIONS
Headline Book Publishing Managing Director *Martin Neild*; IMPRINTS
Headline; Review.
Hodder & Stoughton General Managing Director *Jamie Hodder-Williams*
IMPRINTS **Hodder & Stoughton; Lir; Coronet; Flame; New English Library;**
Sceptre; Mobius.
Hodder Children's Books Managing Director *Charles Nettleton* IMPRINTS
Hodder Children's Books; Signature; Bite; Wayland. CHILDREN'S AUTHORS
David Almond, Dawn Apperley, Colin Bateman, Malorie Blackman, Nick
Butterworth, Kathryn Cave, Lauren Child, Bruce Coville, Cressida Cowell,
Lucy Daniels, Paula Danziger, Sam Godwin, Kes Gray, Mick Inkpen, Robin
Jarvis, Penny Little, Geraldine McCaughrean, Hilary McKay, David Melling,
Michael Morpurgo, Jenny Oldfield, Kenneth Oppel, Christopher Pike, Bali

Rai, Michael Rosen, Shoo Rayner, Tony Ross, Margaret Ryan, Emma Thomson, Ian Whybrow.

Hodder & Stoughton Religious Managing Director *Charles Nettleton* IMPRINTS **Hodder & Stoughton**; **Hodder Christian Books**; **Help Yourself**. **Hodder Education** Managing Director *Philip Walters* Publishes in the following areas: **Schoolbooks** *Lis Tribe*; **Consumer Education** *Katie Roden*; **Further Education/Higher Education Textbooks** *Mary Attree*; **Health Sciences** *Georgina Bentliff*; **Journals/Reference Books** *Mary Attree*. IMPRINTS **Hodder Murray**; **Teach Yourself**; **Hodder Arnold** *John Murray* (Educational).

Honno Welsh Women's Press

c/o Canolfan Merched y Wawr, Vulcan Street, Aberystwyth
SY23 1JH
☎ 01970 623150   Fax 01970 623150
Email post@honno.co.uk
Website www.honno.co.uk

Editor *Lindsay Ashford*

FOUNDED in 1986 by a group of women who wanted to create more opportunities for women in publishing. A co-operative operation which publishes fiction (adult and teenage) and children's books, all with a Welsh connection. Also publishes poetry, short story and autobiographical anthologies. CHILDREN'S AUTHORS Alys Jones, Anne Lewis, Jenny Marlowe, Merryn Williams. Welcomes mss and ideas for books from women only. All material must have a Welsh connection and be sent as hard copy, not by email.

John Hunt Publishing Ltd

46a West Street, New Alresford SO24 9AU
☎ 01962 736880   Fax 01962 736881
Email maria@johnhunt-publishing.com
Website www.johnhunt-publishing.com
Website www.o-books.net

Approx. Annual Turnover £1.5 million

Publishes children's and world religions as well as mind, body & spirit titles. About 25 a year. IMPRINTS **Hunt & Thorpe; John Hunt Publishing; Arthur James; O Books**. CHILDREN'S AUTHORS Andrew Bianchi, Bob Bond, Nick Butterworth, Meryl Doney, Jo Glen, Veronica Heley, Mick Inkpen, Michael Keene, Linda and Alan Parry, Rhona Pipe, Eira Reeves, Andy Robb, Peter Rogers, Fay Sampson, Russell Stannard, Prue Theobalds, Sarah Thorley, Marneta Viegas, Mark Water, Karen Whiting, John Woolley. Unsolicited material welcome.

Icon Books

Grange Road, Duxford, Cambridge CB2 4QF

☎ 01763 208008   Fax 01763 208080

Email info@iconbooks.co.uk

Website www.iconbooks.co.uk

Managing Director *Peter Pugh*
Editorial Director *Richard Appignanesi*
Publishing Director *Jeremy Cox*

FOUNDED 1992. Publishes 'provocative and intelligent' non-fiction in science, politics and philosophy. IMPRINT **Wizard Books** Children's fiction and non-fiction including SERIES *Fighting Fantasy* (adventure game books). CHILDREN'S AUTHORS Garry Chalk, Steve Jackson, Ian Livingstone, Diane Redmond, Jon Sutherland. Submit synopsis only.

Kingfisher Publications Plc

New Penderel House, 283–288 High Holborn, London WC1V 7HZ

☎ 020 7903 9999   Fax 020 7242 4979

Email sales@kingfisherpub.com

Managing Director *John Richards*

Formerly Larousse plc until 1997 when the company name changed to Kingfisher Publications Plc. FOUNDED 1994 when owners, Groupe de la Cité (also publishers of the Larousse dictionaries in France), merged their

UK operations of Grisewood & Dempsey and **Chambers Harrap Publishers Ltd**. In 2002, Kingfisher officially became an imprint of **Houghton Mifflin Company**. DIVISION **Kingfisher** Non-fiction Publishing Director *Gill Denton* FOUNDED in 1973 by Grisewood & Dempsey Ltd. Publishes children's fiction and non-fiction in hardback and paperback: story books, rhymes and picture books, fiction and poetry anthologies, young non-fiction, activity books, general series and reference. CHILDREN'S AUTHORS Alan Baker, Edward & Nancy Bishen, Tony Bradman, Lynn Breeze, Joyce Lankester Brisley, Alan Durant, Rebecca Elgar, Vivian French, Sally Grindley, Sue Heap, Judy Hindley, Anthony Horowitz, Linda Jennings, Anthony Masters, Roger McGough, Jane Olliver, Richard Platt, Colin West, Robert Westall, Ian Whybrow, Jacqueline Wilson, Frieda Wishinsky. No unsolicited mss accepted.

Frances Lincoln Ltd
4 Torriano Mews, Torriano Avenue, London
☎ 020 7284 4009   Fax 020 7267 5249
Email firstname and initial of surname@frances-lincoln.com
Website www.franceslincoln.com

Managing Director *John Nicoll*

FOUNDED 1977. Publishes highly illustrated non-fiction: gardening, art and interiors, health, crafts, children's picture and information books; and stationery. DIVISIONS **Adult Non-fiction** *Jo Christian*; **Children's General Fiction and Non-fiction** *Janetta Otter-Barry*. CHILDREN'S AUTHORS Scoular Anderson, Jane Andrews, Laurence and Catherine Anholt, Chris Baines, Christina Balit, Pauline Baynes, David Bellamy, Lauren Child, Wendy Cooling, Prodeepta Das, Niki Daly, Terrance Dicks, Jill Dow, Berlie Doherty, Malachy Doyle, Opal Dunn, Fiona French, Sarah Garland, Adèle Geras, Debi Gliori, Sally Grindley, Sue Hellard, Kathy Henderson, Mary Hoffman, Meredith Hooper, Richard Kidd, Debbie MacKinnon, Eric Maddern, Mick Manning and Brita Granstorm, Roger McGough, Michael Morpurgo, Anna Obiols, Ifeoma Onyefulu, Jan Ormerod, M. P. Robertson,

Jessica Souhami, Steve Weatherill, Jacqueline Wilson, Jakki Wood, Benjamin Zephaniah, Jonny Zucker. Synopses and ideas for books considered.

Lion Publishing

Mayfield House, 256 Banbury Road, Oxford OX2 7DH

☎ 01865 302750   Fax 01865 302757

Email enquiry@lion-publishing.co.uk

Website www.lion-publishing.co.uk

Managing Director *Paul Clifford*

Approx. Annual Turnover £6.77 million

FOUNDED 1971. A Christian book publisher, strong on illustrated books for a popular international readership, with rights sold in over 100 languages worldwide. Publishes a diverse list with Christian viewpoint the common denominator. All ages, from board books for children to multi-contributor adult reference, educational, paperbacks and colour co-editions and gift books. DIVISIONS **Adult** *Laura Derico;* **Children's and Giftlines** *Catherine Giddings.* CHILDREN'S AUTHORS Su Box, Hilary Brand, Paul Cookson, Pauline Fisk, Penny Frank, Meg Harper, Bob Hartman, Stewart Henderson, Mary Joslin, Stephen Lawhead, Sue Mayfield, Geraldine McCaughrean, Roger McGough, Ann Pilling, Sophie Piper, Lois Rock, Avril Rowlands, Fay Sampson, Steve Turner, Bett Webb. Unsolicited mss accepted provided they have a positive Christian viewpoint intended for a wide general and international readership.

Little Tiger Press

An imprint of Magi Publications, 1 The Coda Centre, 189 Munster Road, London SW6 6AW

☎ 020 7385 6333   Fax 020 7385 7333

Email info@littletiger.co.uk

Website www.littletigerpress.com

Publisher *Monty Bhatia*

Editor *Jude Evans*

Approx. Annual Turnover £4.5 million

Publishes children's picture and novelty books for ages 0–7. No texts over 750 words. CHILDREN'S AUTHORS Klaus Baumgart, David Bedford, Michael Catchpool, Christyan and Diane Fox, Claire Freedman, Ruth Galloway, Gaby Hansen, Nicola Grant, Diana Hendry, Jane Johnson, Christine Leeson, Amanda Leslie, Sam Lloyd, Alan MacDonald, Liz Pichon, David Roberts, Julie Sykes, Debbie Tarbett Catherine Walters, Nick Ward, Tim Warnes. Unsolicited mss, synopses and new ideas welcome. See website for submission guidelines.

The Lutterworth Press

PO Box 60, Cambridge CB1 2NT

☎ 01223 350865   Fax 01223 366951

Email publishing@lutterworth.com

Website www.lutterworth.com

Managing Director *Adrian Brink*

The Lutterworth Press dates back to the 18th century when it was founded by the Religious Tract Society. In the 19th century it was best known for its children's books and magazines, both religious and secular, including *The Boys' Own Paper*. Since 1984 it has been an imprint of **James Clarke & Co.** Publishes religious books for adults and children, adult non-fiction, children's fiction and non-fiction. Approach in writing with ideas in the first instance.

Macmillan Publishers Ltd

The Macmillan Building, 4 Crinan Street, London N1 9XW

☎ 020 7833 4000   Fax 020 7843 4640

Website www.macmillan.com

Chief Executive *Richard Charkin*

Approx. Annual Turnover £300 million (Book Publishing Group)

FOUNDED 1843. Macmillan is one of the largest publishing houses in Britain, publishing approximately 1400 titles a year. In 1995, Verlagsgruppe Georg von Holtzbrinck, a major German publisher, acquired a majority stake in the Macmillan Group. In 1996, Macmillan bought Boxtree, the successful media tie-in publisher and, in 1997, purchased the Heinemann English language teaching list from Reed Elsevier. No unsolicited material. DIVISIONS

Palgrave Macmillan Brunel Road, Houndmills, Basingstoke, Hampshire RG21 6XS ☎01256 329242 Fax 01256 479476 Managing Director *Dominic Knight*; **College** *Frances Arnold*; **Scholarly & Reference** *Sam Burridge*; **Journals** *David Bull*. Publishes textbooks, monographs and journals in academic and professional subjects. Publications in both hard copy and electronic format.

Macmillan Education Macmillan Oxford, 4 Between Towns Road, Oxford OX4 3PP ☎01865 405700 Fax 01865 405701 Email: info@macmillan.com Website www.macmillaneducation.com Executive Chairman *Christopher Paterson*; Managing Director *Chris Harrison*; Publishing Directors *Sue Bale* (ELT), *Alison Hubert* (Education), *Ian Johnstone* (Internet). Publishes a wide range of ELT titles and educational materials for the international education market from Oxford and through 30 subsidiaries worldwide.

Pan Macmillan 20 New Wharf Road, London N1 9RR ☎020 7014 6000 Fax 020 7014 6001 www.panmacmillan.com Managing Director *David North*. Publishes under **Macmillan, Pan, Picador, Sidgwick & Jackson, Boxtree, Macmillan Children's Books, Campbell Books.**
IMPRINTS

Macmillan (founded 1843) Fiction: Publishing Director *Maria Rejt*, Editorial Director *Imogen Taylor* Publishes hardback commercial and literary fiction including genre fiction, romantic, crime and thrillers. IMPRINT **Tor** (founded 2003) Editorial Director *Peter Lavery* Publishes science fiction, fantasy and thrillers. Non-Fiction: Publisher *Richard Milner*, Editorial Director *Georgina Morley* Publishes serious and general non-fiction: autobiography, biography, economics, history, philosophy, politics and world affairs, psychology, popular science, trade reference titles.

Pan (founded 1947) Paperback imprint for Pan Macmillan.

Picador (founded 1972) Publisher *Andrew Kidd*, Senior Editorial Director *Ursula Doyle*. Publishes literary international fiction and non-fiction.

Sidgwick & Jackson (founded 1908) Publishes popular non-fiction in hardback and trade paperback with strong personality or marketable identity, from celebrity and showbusiness to music and sport. Also military history list.

Boxtree (founded 1986) Publishes brand and media tie-in titles, including TV, film, music and Internet, plus entertainment licences, pop culture, humour and event-related books.

Macmillan Children's Books (New Wharf Road address) Managing Director *Kate Wilson*; **Fiction, Non-Fiction, Poetry** *Sarah Davies*; **Picture Books and Gift Books** *Suzanne Carnell*; **Campbell Books** *Camilla Reid*. IMPRINTS **Macmillan, Pan, Campbell Books, Young Picador.** Publishes novels, board books, picture books, non-fiction (illustrated and non-illustrated), poetry and novelty books in paperback and hardback. CHILDREN'S AUTHORS James Berry, Julie Bertagna, Terence Blacker, Valerie Bloom, Judy Blume, Georgia Byng, Meg Cabot, Rod Campbell, Charles Causley, Paul Cookson, Peter Dickinson, Carol Ann Duffy, Lian Hearn, Eve Ibbotson, Jenny Joseph, Elizabeth Laird, Lydia Monks, Brian Moses, Jill Murphy, Gareth Owen, Gwyneth Rees, Axel Scheffler, Nick Sharratt, Roger Stevens, Paul Stewart and Chris Riddell, Nick Toczek, Robert Westall, Ian Whybrow, Jeanne Willis.

Kevin Mayhew Publishers

Buxhall, Stowmarket, Suffolk IP14 3BW
☎01449 737978   Fax 01449 737834
Email info@kevinmayhewltd.com
Website www.kevinmayhewltd.com

Chairman *Kevin Mayhew*
Managing Director *Gordon Carter*
Commissioning Editors *Kevin Mayhew, Jonathan Bugden*

FOUNDED in 1976. One of the leading sacred music and Christian book publishers in the UK. Publishes religious titles – liturgy, sacramental, devotional, also children's books and school resources. IMPRINT **Palm Tree Press** Worldwide worship. CHILDREN'S AUTHORS Michael Forster, Bernard Foster and David Gatward, Clare Freedman and Arthur Baker, Heather Henning,

Dave and Lynn Hopwood, Graham Jeffery, Patricia Jones. Unsolicited synopses and mss welcome; telephone prior to sending material, please.

Meadowside Children's Books

185 Fleet Street, London EC4A 2HS
☎ 020 7400 1087   Fax 020 7400 1037
Email info@meadowsidebooks.com
Website www.meadowsidebooks.com

Chairman *Mark Battles*
Managing Director *Simon Rosenheim*
Editorial Manager *Alison Maloney*
Approx. Annual Turnover £1.4 million

FOUNDED in September 2003 by D.C. Thomson. Publishes pre-school picture, novelty and early learning books. Unsolicited mss, synopses and ideas welcome. Send to the Editorial Department by mail or email.

Milet Publishing Limited

6 North End Parade, London W14 0SJ
☎ 020 7603 5477   Fax 020 7610 5475
Email info@milet.com
Website www.milet.com

Managing Directors *Sedat Turhan, Patricia Billings*

FOUNDED 1995. Publishes children's picture books in English and dual language; world literature for adults and language books. DIVISIONS **Children's, English**; **Children's, Dual Language** *Patricia Billings* CHILDREN'S AUTHORS Alison Boyle, Helen Cowcher, Laura Hambleton, David McKee, Mandy & Ness, Jane Simmons, Tracy V. Spates, Gwenyth Swain. **World Literature**; **Language Books** *Sedat Turhan*. Welcomes synopses and ideas for books. Send proposal, outline or synopsis with sample text and/or artwork, by post only. 'Please review submission guidelines and existing titles on our website before submitting. We like bold, original stories and artwork, universal and/or multicultural.'

National Trust Publications

36 Queen Anne's Gate, London SW1H 9AS

☎ 020 7222 9251   Fax 020 7222 5097

Website www.nationaltrust.org.uk

Chairman *Sir William Proby*
Director-General *Fiona Reynolds*
Publisher *Margaret Willes*

Publishing arm of The National Trust, founded in 1895 by Robert Hunter, Octavia Hill and Hardwicke Rawnsley to protect and conserve places of historic interest and beauty. Publishes gardening, cookery, handbooks, social history, architecture, general interest and children's books. CHILDREN'S AUTHORS Paul Dowswell, Jen Green, Cathy Lewis, James Parry. No unsolicited material.

Michael O'Mara Books Ltd

9 Lion Yard, Tremadoc Road, London SW4 7NQ

☎ 020 7720 8643   Fax 020 7627 8953

Email firstname.lastname@michaelomarabooks.com

Website www.mombooks.com

Chairman *Michael O'Mara*
Managing Director *Lesley O'Mara*
Editorial Director (Commissioning) *Lindsay Davies*
Approx. Annual Turnover £5 million

FOUNDED 1985. Independent publisher. Publishes general non-fiction, royalty, history, humour, children's novelties, anthologies and reference. IMPRINT **Buster Books** Children's titles. CHILDREN'S AUTHORS Jo Brown, Michelle Cartlidge, Rachael O'Neill, Tim Weare, Hans Wilhelm. Unsolicited mss, synopses and ideas for books welcome.

The Orion Publishing Group Limited

Orion House, 5 Upper St Martin's Lane, London WC2H 9EA
☎ 020 7240 3444   Fax 020 7240 4822
Website www.orionbooks.co.uk/pub/index.htm

Chairman *Arnaud Nourry*
Chief Executive *Peter Roche*
Deputy Chief Executive *Malcolm Edwards*
Approx. Annual Turnover £70 million

FOUNDED 1992 by Anthony Cheetham, Rosemary Cheetham and Peter Roche. Incorporates Weidenfeld & Nicolson, JM Dent, Chapmans Publishers and Cassell. DIVISIONS **Orion** Managing Director *Malcolm Edwards* IMPRINTS **Orion Fiction; Orion Media; Orion Children's** Publisher *Fiona Kennedy* Children's fiction/non-fiction. CHILDREN'S AUTHORS Kevin Crossley-Holland, Sally Gardner, Alan Gibbons, Francesca Simon. **Gollancz. Weidenfeld & Nicolson** Managing Director *Adrian Bourne* IMPRINTS **Weidenfeld Illustrated; Weidenfeld General; Phoenix Press; Cassell Reference; Cassell Military; Custom Publishing. Paperback Division** Managing Director *Susan Lamb* IMPRINTS **Orion; Phoenix; Everyman.**

Oxford University Press

Great Clarendon Street, Oxford OX2 6DP
☎ 01865 556767   Fax 01865 556646
Email enquiry@oup.com
Website www.oup.com

Chief Executive *Henry Reece*
Approx. Annual Turnover £392 million

A department of Oxford University, OUP started as the university's printing business and developed into a major publishing operation in the 19th century. Publishes academic works in all formats (print and online): dictionaries, lexical and non-lexical reference, scholarly journals, student texts, schoolbooks, ELT materials, music, bibles, paperbacks, and children's books.

CHILDREN'S AUTHORS Rachel Anderson, Quentin Blake, Michael Bond, Gillian Cross, Adèle Geras, Diana Wynne Jones, Geraldine McCaughrean.
DIVISIONS **Academic** *T.M. Barton* Academic and higher education titles in major disciplines, dictionaries (acquired *The Grove Dictionary of Music* in 2003), non-lexical reference, journals and trade books. OUP welcomes first-class academic material in the form of proposals or accepted theses. **Education** *K. Harris* National Curriculum courses and support materials as well as children's literature. **ELT** *P.R.C. Marshall* ELT courses and dictionaries for all levels.

Penguin Group (UK)

A Pearson Company, 80 Strand, London WC2R ORL
☎ 020 7010 3000   Fax 020 7010 6060
Website www.penguin.co.uk

Group Chairman & Chief Executive *John Makinson*
CEO: Penguin UK, Dorling Kindersley Ltd *Anthony Forbes Watson*
Managing Director: Penguin *Helen Fraser*
Approx. Annual Turnover £121 million

Owned by Pearson plc. The world's best known book brand and for more than 60 years a leading publisher whose adult and children's lists include fiction, non-fiction, poetry, drama, classics, reference and special interest areas. Reprints and new work.
DIVISIONS
Penguin General Books Managing Director *Tom Weldon* Adult fiction and non-fiction is published in hardback under **Michael Joseph**, **Viking** and **Hamish Hamilton** IMPRINTS. Paperbacks come under the Penguin imprint.
Penguin Press Managing Director *Stefan* IMPRINTS **Allen Lane**; **Penguin Reference**. No unsolicited mss.
Frederick Warne Managing Director *Sally Floyer* Classic children's publishing and merchandising including *Beatrix Potter; Flower Fairies; Orlando.*
Ventura Publisher *Sally Floyer* Producer and packager of *Spot* titles by Eric Hill.
Ladybird (see **Dorling Kindersley Ltd**).

BBC Children's Books *Sally Floyer* New imprint launched in 2004.
Puffin Managing Director *Francesca Dow* (poetry and picture books) Publishers *Rebecca McNally* (fiction), *Clare Hulton* (media and popular non-fiction). Leading children's paperback list, publishing in virtually all fields including fiction, non-fiction, poetry, picture books, media-related titles. CHILDREN'S AUTHORS Allan Ahlberg, Nina Bawden, Melvin Burgess, Eric Carle, Eoin Colfer, Susan Cooper, Berlie Doherty, Anne Fine, Susan Gates, Morris Gleitzman, Harry Horse, Brian Jacques, Pete Johnson, Terry Jones, Dick King-Smith, Joan Lingard, Brian Patten, Philippa Pearce, Gervase Phinn, Jan Pienkowski, Chris Riddell, Philip Ridley, Michael Rosen, Jeremy Strong, Kaye Umansky.
No unsolicited mss; synopses and ideas welcome.

Piccadilly Press

5 Castle Road, London NW1 8PR
☎020 7267 4492   Fax 020 7267 4493
Email books@piccadillypress.co.uk
Website www.piccadillypress.co.uk
Publisher/Managing Director *Brenda Gardner*
Approx. Annual Turnover £1.4 million

FOUNDED 1983. Independent publisher of children's and parental books. CHILDREN'S AUTHORS Jane Andrews, Sally Chambers, Simon Cheshire, Fran Evans, John Farman, Sue Hellard, Cathy Hopkins, Kathryn Lamb, Tony Maddox, Nadia Marks, Frank McGinty, Moira Munro, Louise Rennison, Rosie Rushton, Lisa Stubbs, Lynda Waterhouse, Cherry Whytock. Welcomes approaches from authors 'but we would like them to know the sort of books we do. It is frustrating to get inappropriate material. They should check in their local libraries, bookshops or look at our website. We will send a catalogue (please enclose s.a.e.).' No adult or cartoon-type material.

Pinwheel Limited

Winchester House, 259–269 Old Marylebone Road, London NW1 5XJ

☎ 020 7616 7200   Fax 020 7616 7201

Managing Director *Andrew Flatt*

Children's non-fiction, picture books and novelty titles. IMPRINTS **Andromeda Children's Books** Publishing/Creative Director *Linda Cole* Illustrated non-fiction for children from 3–12 years; **Gullane Children's Books** Creative Director *Paula Burgess* Picture books for children from 0–8 years; **Pinwheel Children's Books** Publishing/Creative Director *Linda Cole* Cloth and novelty books for children from 0–5 years. CHILDREN'S AUTHORS Tony Bonning, Jane Cabrera, Lynne Chapman, Sally Crabtree, Joyce Dunbar, Marie-Louise Fitzpatrick, Vivian French, Charles Fuge, Sally Grindley, Simone Lia, Sam Lloyd, Angela McAllister, Charles Middleton, Miriam Moss, Francesca Simon, Carrie Weston, Ian Whybrow, Jude Wisdom, David Wojtowycz. Unsolicited mss will not be returned.

Prestel Publishing Limited

4 Bloomsbury Place, London WC1A 2QA

☎ 020 7323 5004   Fax 020 7636 8004

Email sales@prestel-uk.co.uk

Website www.prestel.com

Chairman *Jürgen Tesch*

FOUNDED 1924. Publishes art, architecture, photography, children's and general illustrated books. No fiction. Unsolicited mss, synopses and ideas welcome. Approach by post or email.

The Random House Group Ltd

Random House, 20 Vauxhall Bridge Road, London SW1V 2SA

☎ 020 7840 8400   Fax 020 7233 6058

Email enquiries@randomhouse.co.uk

Website www.randomhouse.co.uk

Chief Executive/Chairman *Gail Rebuck*
Deputy Chairman *Simon Master*
Managing Director *Ian Hudson*

The Random House Group is the UK's leading trade publisher comprising 31 diverse imprints in four separate substantially autonomous divisions: the Random House Division, Ebury Press, Transworld and Random House Children's Books. Acquired The Harvill Press in 2002 and C.W. Daniel in March 2004.

RANDOM HOUSE DIVISION
IMPRINTS **Jonathan Cape Ltd; Yellow Jersey Press; Harvill Secker; Chatto & Windus; Pimlico; Vintage; Century; William Heinemann; Hutchinson. Random House Business Books. Arrow.**

EBURY PRESS DIVISION
☎020 7840 8400   Fax 020 7840 8406 Publisher *Fiona MacIntyre* IMPRINTS **Ebury Press; Vermilion; Rider; Fodors**.

RANDOM HOUSE CHILDREN'S BOOKS (at Transworld Publishers, 61–63 Uxbridge Road, London W5 5SA   ☎020 8231 6800   Fax 020 8231 6767) Managing Director *Philippa Dickinson* IMPRINTS **Hutchinson** Publishing Director *Caroline Roberts*; **Jonathan Cape; The Bodley Head; Doubleday Picture Books** Publisher *Penny Walker*; **David Fickling Books** Publishing Director *David Fickling*, Fiction Publisher *Annie Eaton*; **Corgi; Red Fox**. CHILDREN'S AUTHORS Joan Aitken, Nicholas Allan, Giles Andreae, Malorie Blackman, Raymond Briggs, John Burningham, Caroline Castle, Rob Childs, Babette Cole, Ted Dewan, Chris d'Lacey, Catherine Fisher, Adele Geras, Keith Gray, Kes Gray, Mark Haddon, Mairi Hedderwick, Jane Hissey, Brian Jacques, Satoshi Kitamura, Jan Mark, Simon Mason, David McKee, Robin McKinley, Tony Mitton, Christopher Paolini, Terry Pratchett, Philip Pullman, S. F. Said, Nick Sharratt, Helen Stephens, Paul Stewart and Chris Riddell, Nick Ward, Robert Westall, Jacqueline Wilson. Unsolicited mss, synopses and ideas for books welcome.

Ransom Publishing Ltd

Rose Cottage, Howe Hill, Watlington OX49 5HB

☎ 01491 613711   Fax 01491 613733

Email jenny@ransom.co.uk

Website www.ransom.co.uk

Managing Director *Jenny Ertle*

FOUNDED 1995 by ex-McGraw-Hill publisher. Partnerships formed with, among others, Channel 4 and the ICL. Publishes educational and consumer multimedia, study packs and children's books. CHILDREN'S AUTHORS Toni McKay-Lawton, Diane Napier, Steve Rickard, Jenny Warland. Unlikely to take new submissions this year though may consider storybooks and grammar books for primary education. Ransom is looking for banks of questions for primary and secondary geography and science.

Saint Andrew Press

Church of Scotland, 121 George Street, Edinburgh EH2 4YN

☎ 0131 225 5722   Fax 0131 220 3113

Email standrewpress@cofscotland.org.uk

Website www.standrewpress.com

Website www.williambarclay.org

Head of Publishing *Ann Crawford*

Approx. Annual Turnover £225,000

FOUNDED in 1954. Owned by the Church of Scotland. Publishes religious, general reference and children's books aimed at the Christian trade and retail market in the UK and internationally. CHILDREN'S AUTHORS Russell Deal, Susie Poole, Kenneth Steven, Tom White. 'Saint Andrew Press is expanding and is actively seeking high-quality writing that is thought-provoking and, above all, helps readers to wrestle with the complexities of life today.' No unsolicited mss but proposals very welcome in synopsis form; approach in writing.

Scholastic Ltd

Villiers House, Clarendon Avenue, Leamington Spa CV32 5PR
☎ 01926 887799   Fax 01926 883331
Website www.scholastic.co.uk

Chairman *M.R. Robinson*
Managing Director *To be appointed*
Approx. Annual Turnover £42 million

FOUNDED 1964. Owned by US parent company. Publishes children's fiction and non-fiction and education for primary schools. CHILDREN'S AUTHORS Tony Abbott, Ian Beck, Elizabeth Bennett, Keith Brumpton, Anne Cassidy, Martin Chatterton, Michael Coleman, Trish Cook, Jo Davies, Terry Deary, Penny Dolan, Helen Dunmore, Gregg Gormley, Simon Goswell, Mary Hooper, Karen McCombie, Liz Mills, Liz Pichon, Dav Pilkey, Philip Pullman, Catherine Robinson, Emily Rodda, Maureen Roffey, Nick Sharratt, Alan Temperley, James Thomas, Pat Thomson, Kaye Umansky, Eleanor Updale, Nick Ward, Holly Webb.

DIVISIONS **Scholastic Children's Books** *Richard Scrivener* Commonwealth House, 1–19 New Oxford Street, London WC1A 1NU   ☎ 020 7421 9000   Fax 020 7421 9001 IMPRINTS **Scholastic Press** (hardbacks); **Hippo** (paperbacks); **Point** (paperbacks) TITLES *Horrible Histories; Goosebumps; Point Horror; His Dark Materials* trilogy by Philip Pullman.

Educational Publishing *Max Adam* (Villiers House address) Professional books and classroom materials for primary teachers, plus magazines such as *Child Education, Junior Education, Junior Focus, Infant Projects, Nursery Education; Literacy Time.*

Scholastic Book Clubs *Miles Stevens Hoare* Windrush Park, Witney, Oxford OX29 0YT   ☎ 01993 893456   Fax 01993 776813 SBC is the UK's number one Schools Book Club. Offering five age specific clubs, it provides 'the best books at great prices and supports teachers in the process'.

School Book Fairs *Miles Stevens-Hoare* The Book Fair Division sells directly to children, parents and teachers in schools through 27,000 week-long book events held in schools throughout the UK.

Scottish Cultural Press/Scottish Children's Press

Unit 6, Newbattle Abbey Business Park, Newbattle Road, Dalkeith
EH22 3LJ
☎ 0131 660 6366   Fax 0131 660 4666
Email info@scottishbooks.com
Website www.scottishbooks.com

Directors *Avril Gray, Brian Pugh*

FOUNDED 1992. Publishes Scottish interest titles, including cultural literature, poetry, archaeology, local history. DIVISION **S.C.P. Children's Ltd** (trading as **Scottish Children's Press**) Children's fiction and non-fiction. CHILDREN'S AUTHORS Liz Ashworth, Theresa Breslin, Marit Brunskill, A. D. Cameron, Ian Cameron, Allan Campbell, Marion Campbell, Thomas Chalmers, Neil & Elizabeth Curtis, Sheila Douglas, Anne Forsyth, Alan Hemus, Margharita Hughes, Antony Kamm, Donald Lightwood, James McGonigal, Stuart McHardy, Bernard MacLaverty, Moira Miller, Eileen Ramsay, William J. Rae, Dilys Rose, Kendrick Ross, Sylvia Turtle, Samantha Valentine, Hamish Whyte. Unsolicited mss, synopses and ideas accepted provided return postage is included, but *always* telephone before sending material, please. 'Mss sent without advance telephone call and return postage will be destroyed.'

Short Books

15 Highbury Terrace, London N5 1UP
☎ 020 7226 1607   Fax 020 7226 4169
Email mark@shortbooks.biz
Website www.theshortbookco.com

Contacts *Rebecca Nicolson, Aurea Carpenter*

FOUNDED 2001. Publishes informative, entertaining non-fiction (30,000–80,000 words), mainly biography and journalism; authors include Francis Wheen, Nicci Gerrard, Ferdinand Mount and Simon Barnes. Children's books (15,000–20,000 words): lively biographies of famous figures from the past. CHILDREN'S AUTHORS Laura Beatty, Andrew Billen, Charlie Boxer,

Rupert Christiansen, Claudia Fitzherbert, Adrian Hadland, Kate Hubbard, Lucy Lethbridge, Sam Llewellyn, Neil Middleton, Amanda Mitchison, Charlotte Moore, Neil Stroud, Tony Thorne. No fiction as yet but always open to new ideas. 'All prospective authors will be informed by email of how their proposal has been received. Mss will not be returned.'

Snowbooks Ltd

239 Old Street, London EC1V 9EY
☎ 020 7553 4473   Fax 020 7251 3130
Email editor@snowbooks.com
Website www.snowbooks.com

Managing Director *Emma Cahill*
Approx. Annual Turnover £200,000

FOUNDED 2003. Publishes fiction mainly (both contemporay and classics) but also considers fiction and poetry, non-fiction, humour, children's, business, crime, mystery, travel, general interest, biography and autobiography. No romance, science fiction, mind body and spirit, religious books. Unsolicited synopses and ideas for books welcome provided a sample of writing is attached. Approach by email in the first instance.

Souvenir Press Ltd

43 Great Russell Street, London WC1B 3PA
☎ 020 7580 9307/8 & 7637 5711/2/3   Fax 020 7580 5064
Email souvenirpress@ukonline.co.uk

Chairman/Managing Director *Ernest Hecht*

Independent publishing house. FOUNDED 1951. Publishes academic and scholarly, animal care and breeding, antiques and collecting, archaeology, autobiography and biography, business and industry, children's, cookery, crafts and hobbies, crime, educational, fiction, gardening, health and beauty, history and antiquarian, humour, illustrated and fine editions, magic and the occult, medical, military, music, natural history, philosophy, poetry, psychology, religious, sociology, sports, theatre and women's studies. Souvenir's Human Horizons series for the disabled and their carers is one of the most pre-eminent in its field and recently celebrated 28 years of publishing for the disabled. IMPRINTS/SERIES **Condor; Human Horizons; Independent Voices; Pictorial Presentations; Pop Universal; The Story-Tellers**. Unsolicited mss considered but initial letter of enquiry and outline always required in the first instance.

Tango Books Ltd
3D West Point, 36–37 Warple Way, London W3 0RG
☎ 020 8996 9970   Fax 020 8996 9977
Email sales@tangobooks.co.uk

Directors *David Fielder, Sheri Safran*

FOUNDED 1981. Children's books publisher with international co-edition potential: pop-ups, three-dimensional, novelty, picture and board books, 1000 words maximum. Approach with preliminary letter and sample material in the first instance.

Time Warner Books UK
Brettenham House, Lancaster Place, London WC2E 7EN
☎ 020 7911 8000   Fax 020 7911 8100
Email uk@twbg.co.uk
Website www.TimeWarnerBooks.co.uk

Chief Executive *David Young*
Publisher *Ursula Mackenzie*
Approx. Annual Turnover £40 million

FOUNDED 1988 as Little, Brown & Co. (UK). Part of Time Warner. Began by importing its US parent company's titles and in 1990 launched its own illustrated non-fiction list. Two years later the company took over former Macdonald & Co. Publishes hardback and paperback fiction, literary fiction, crime, science fiction and fantasy; and general non-fiction including true crime, biography and autobiography, cinema, gardening, history, humour, popular science, travel, reference, cookery, wines and spirits. IMPRINTS

Little, Brown *Ursula Mackenzie, Richard Beswick, Barbara Daniel, Hilary Hale, Tara Lawrence* Hardback fiction and general non-fiction; **Abacus** *Richard Beswick* Literary fiction and non-fiction paperbacks; **Atom** *Darren Nash* Young adult/teen paperbacks; **Orbit** *Tim Holman* Science fiction and fantasy; **Time Warner** *Tara Lawrence, Barbara Daniel, Hilary Hale* Mass-market fiction and non-fiction hardbacks and paperbacks; **X Libris** *Sarah Shrubb* Women's erotica; **Virago Press**. Approach in writing in the first instance. No unsolicited mss.

Usborne Publishing Ltd

83–85 Saffron Hill, London EC1N 8RT
☎ 020 7430 2800   Fax 020 7430 1562
Email mail@usborne.co.uk
Website www.usborne.com

Managing Director *Peter Usborne*
Publishing Director *Jenny Tyler*
Approx. Annual Turnover £20 million

FOUNDED 1973. Publishes non-fiction, fiction, art and activity books, puzzle books and music for children, young adults and pre-school. Some titles for parents. Up to 250 titles a year. CHILDREN'S AUTHORS Lloyd Alexander, Bowvayne, Ann Bryant, Terry Deary, Ann Evans, Adèle Geras, Sandra Glover, Diana Kimpton, Linda Newbery, Rodman Philbrick, Malcolm Rose, Paul Stewart, Ann Turnbull. Non-fiction books are written in-house to a specific format and therefore unsolicited mss are not normally welcome. Ideas which may be developed in-house are sometimes considered. Fiction for children will be considered. Keen to hear from new illustrators and designers.

Walker Books Ltd

87 Vauxhall Walk, London SE11 5HJ
☎ 020 7793 0909   Fax 020 7587 1123

Email editorial@walker.co.uk
Website www.walkerbooks.co.uk

Publisher *Jane Winterbotham*
Editorial Director *Gill Evans*
Editors *Deirdre McDermott* (picture books), *Caroline Royds* (fiction, non-fiction and gift books), *Denise Johnstone-Burt* (picture books, board and novelty), *Lorraine Taylor* (character, audio, stationery and merchandising)
Approx. Annual Turnover £31.7 million

FOUNDED 1979. Publishes illustrated children's books, children's fiction and non-fiction. CHILDREN'S AUTHORS Alan Ahlberg, Jez Alborough, Lucy Cousins, Kate DiCamillo, Barbara Firth, Bob Graham, Martin Handford, Sonya Hartnett, Colin and Jacqui Hawkins, Petr Horacek, Anthony Horowitz, Harry Horse, Anita Jeram & Sam McBratney, Dick King-Smith, Jill Murphy, Helen Oxenbury, Chris Riddell and Richard Platt, Martin Waddell.

The Watts Publishing Group Ltd
96 Leonard Street, London EC2A 4XD
☎ 020 7739 2929   Fax 020 7739 2318
Email gm@wattspub.co.uk
Website www.wattspublishing.co.uk

Managing Director *Marlene Johnson*

Part of Groupe Lagardere. Publishes children's non-fiction, reference, information, gift, fiction, picture and novelty books and audio books. IMPRINTS **Franklin Watts** *Philippa Stewart* Non-fiction and information; **Orchard Books** *Ann-Janine Murtagh* Fiction, picture and novelty books. CHILDREN'S AUTHORS Giles Andreae, Laurence and Catherine Anholt, Bernard Ashley, Angela Barrett, Ian Beck, Ann Bryant, John Butler, Lauren Child, Michael Coleman, Penny Dann, Chris d'Lacey, Michael Foreman, Lindsay Gardiner, Debi Gliori, Sally Hewitt, Anthony Horowitz, Rose Impey, Julia Jarman, Brian Keaney, Michael Lawrence, Mick Manning & Brita Granström, Anthony Masters, James Mayhew, Geraldine McCaughrean, Adrian Mitch-

144

ell, Tony Mitton, Pat Moon, Linda Newbury, Guy Parker-Rees, Jane May, Shoo Rayner, Arthur Robins, Jane Simmons, Emily Smith, Jerry Spinelli, Jean Ure, Karen Wallace, David Wojtowycz, Philip Wooderson. Unsolicited material is not considered other than by referral or recommendation.

The Women's Press

27 Goodge Street, London W1T 2LD
☎ 020 7636 3992   Fax 020 7637 1866
Website www.the-womens-press.com

Managing Director *Stella Kane*
Approx. Annual Turnover £1 million

Part of the Namara Group. First title published in 1978. Publishes women only: quality fiction and non-fiction. Fiction usually has a female protagonist and a woman-centred theme. International writers and subject matter encouraged. Non-fiction: books for and about women generally; gender politics, race politics, disability, feminist theory, health and psychology, literary criticism. IMPRINTS **Women's Press Classics; Livewire Books for Teenagers** Fiction and non-fiction series for young adults. Synopses and ideas for books welcome. No mss without previous letter, synopsis and sample material.

The X Press

PO Box 25694, London N17 6FP
☎ 020 8801 2100   Fax 020 8885 1322
Email vibes@xpress.co.uk

Editorial Director *Dotun Adebayo*
Publisher *Steve Pope*

LAUNCHED in 1992 with the cult bestseller *Yardie*, The X Press is the leading publisher of Black-interest fiction in the UK. Also publishes general fiction and children's fiction. IMPRINTS **The X Press; Nia; 20/20.** Send mss rather than synopses or ideas (enclose s.a.e.). No poetry.

Electronic Publishers
with Children's Lists

Deunant Books
PO Box 25, Denbigh LL16 5ZQ
☎ 01745 870259 Fax 01745 870259
Email mail@deunantbooks.com
Website www.deunantbooks.com

Managing Director *Les Broad*

FOUNDED 2001. Internet e-book publisher in English and Welsh of art, biography, children's, comedy, fiction, philosophy, poetry, science fiction, short story compendia, theology, travel. Welcomes written works incorporating video, sound or animation; interactive books, technical manuals.

Online Originals
Priory Cottage, Wordsworth Place, London NW5 4HG
☎ 020 7267 4244
Email editor@onlineoriginals.com
Website www.onlineoriginals.com

Managing Director *David Gettman*
Commissioning Editor *Dr Christopher Macann*

Publishes book-length works on the Internet and as print-on-demand. Acquires global electronic rights (including print-on-demand) in literary fiction, intellectual non-fiction, drama and fiction for young readers (ages 8–16). No poetry, fantasy, how-to, self-help, picture books, cookery, hobbies, crafts or local interest. Unsolicited mss, synopses and ideas for books welcome. *All* authors must have Internet access. Unique peer-review, automated submissions system, accessed via the website address above. Submissions or enquiries on paper or disk will be discarded.

StoryZone Ltd
Ryman's Cottages, Little Tew OX7 4JJ
☎ 0845 458 8408
Email contact@storyzone.co.uk
Website www.storyzone.co.uk

Online children's story library. The website makes available new and published stories by professional writers aimed at children between the ages of 4 and 10. Maximum length 1000 words, with illustrations. Minimum subscription: £5 for 5 stories.

UK Literary Agents for Children's Authors

* = Member of the Association of Authors' Agents

The Agency (London) Ltd*

24 Pottery Lane, London W11 4LZ

☎ 020 7727 1346   Fax 020 7727 9037

Email info@theagency.co.uk

Contacts *Stephen Durbridge, Leah Schmidt, Sebastian Born, Julia Kreitman, Bethan Evans, Hilary Delamere, Katie Haines, Ligeia Marsh, Faye Webber, Nick Quinn*

FOUNDED 1995. Handles writers and rights for TV, film, theatre, radio scripts and children's fiction. Only existing clients for adult fiction or non-fiction. *Commission* Home 10%; US by arrangement. Send letter with s.a.e. No unsolicited mss. No reading fee.

Darley Anderson Literary, TV & Film Agency*

Estelle House, 11 Eustace Road, London SW6 1JB

☎ 020 7385 6652   Fax 020 7386 5571

Email enquiries@darleyanderson.com

Website www.darleyanderson.com

Contacts *Darley Anderson, Lucie Whitehouse* (foreign rights), *Elizabeth Wright* (women's fiction and crime), *Julia Churchill* (children's fiction/non-fiction), *Rosi Bridge* (finance)

Run by an ex-publisher with a sympathetic touch and a knack for spotting talent and making great deals – many for six and seven figure advances. Handles commercial fiction and non-fiction; children's fiction. No academic books or poetry. Special fiction interests: all types of thrillers and crime (American/hard boiled/cosy/historical); women's fiction (sagas, chick-lit, love stories, 'tear jerkers', women in jeopardy) and all types of American and Irish novels. Also comic fiction. Special non-fiction interests: investigative books, revelatory history and science TV tie-ins, celebrity autobiographies, true life women in jeopardy, diet, beauty, health, cookery, popular psychology, self-improvement, inspirational, popular religion and supernatural. *Commission* Home 15%; US & Translation 20%; Film/TV/Radio 20%. Send letter, synopsis and first three chapters; return postage/s.a.e. essential. Disk and emailed submissions cannot be considered.

Author Literary Agents

53 Talbot Road, London N6 4QX
☎ 020 8341 0442/07989 318245 (mobile)   Fax 020 8341 0442
Email agile@authors.co.uk

Contact *John Havergal*

FOUNDED 1997. Thought-through game, toy, animation, picture, graphics and children's concepts for book and screen; also marketed. *Commission* Writing: Home 15%; Overseas & Translation 25%; Non-Writing Media: Publishing or production 25%; advertising one-third. VAT extra. Send half-to-one-page outline plus first chapter/scene/section only for initial appraisal. S.a.e. essential for reply. No reading fee.

The Bell Lomax Agency

James House, 1 Babmaes Street, London SW1Y 6HF
☎ 020 7930 4447   Fax 020 7925 0118
Email agency@bell-lomax.co.uk

Executives *Eddie Bell, Pat Lomax, Paul Moreton, June Bell*

Established 2002. Handles quality fiction and non-fiction, biography, children's, business and sport. No unsolicited mss without preliminary letter. No scripts. No reading fee.

Celia Catchpole

56 Gilpin Avenue, London SW14 8QY

☎ 020 8255 7200   Fax 020 8288 0653

Contact *Celia Catchpole*

FOUNDED 1996. Handles children's books – artists and writers. No TV, film, radio or theatre scripts. No poetry. *Commission* Home 10% (writers) 15% (artists); US & Translation 20%. Works with associate agents abroad. No unsolicited mss.

Conville & Walsh Limited*

2 Ganton Street, London W1F 7QL

☎ 020 7287 3030   Fax 020 7287 4545

Email firstname@convilleandwalsh.com

Directors *Clare Conville, Patrick Walsh* (book rights), *Sam North* (film/TV rights), *Peter Tallack* (popular science)

Established in 2000 by Clare Conville (ex-A.P. Watt) and Patrick Walsh (ex-Christopher Little Literary Agency). Handles literary and commercial fiction plus serious and narrative non-fiction. Clare Conville also represents many successful children's authors. Particularly interested in scientists, historians and journalists. *Commission* Home 15%; US & Translation 20%.

Curtis Brown Group Ltd*

Haymarket House, 28/29 Haymarket, London SW1Y 4SP

☎ 020 7393 4400   Fax 020 7393 4401

Email cb@curtisbrown.co.uk

Group Managing Director *Jonathan Lloyd*
Financial Director *Mark Collingbourne*

Australia: Managing Diector *Fiona Inglis*
Books, London *Jonny Geller, Peter Robinson* (Joint MDs, Books Division), *Jonathan Lloyd, Ali Gunn, Camilla Hornby, Anthea Morton-Saner, Jonathan Pegg, John Saddler, Vivienne Schuster, Janie Swanson, Euan Thorneycroft*

FOUNDED 1899. Agents for the negotiation in all markets of novels, general non-fiction, children's books and associated rights (including multimedia) as well as film, theatre, TV and radio scripts. *Commission* Home 15%; Overseas 20%. Outline for non-fiction and short synopsis for fiction with two – three sample chapters and autobiographical note. No reading fee. Return postage essential.

Caroline Davidson Literary Agency

5 Queen Anne's Gardens, London W4 1TU
☎ 020 8995 5768   Fax 020 8994 2770

Contact *Caroline Davidson*

FOUNDED 1988. Handles fiction and non-fiction, including archaeology, architecture, art, astronomy, biography, design, gardening, health, history, medicine, natural history, reference, science. *Commission* US, Home, Commonwealth, Translation 12½%; 20% if sub-agents are involved. Finished, polished first novels positively welcomed. No occult, short stories, children's, plays or poetry. Writers should send an initial letter giving details of their project and/or book proposal, including the first 50 pages of their novel if a fiction writer, together with c.v. and s.a.e. Submissions without the latter are not considered or returned.

Eddison Pearson Ltd

10 Corinne Road, London N19 5EY
☎ 020 7700 7763   Fax 020 7700 7866
Email info@eddisonpearson.com

Contact *Clare Pearson*

FOUNDED 1995. Handles children's books and scripts, literary fiction and non-fiction, poetry. *Commission* Home 10%; US & Translation 15%. Please enquire in writing, enclosing s.a.e. Email enquiries also welcome. In the first instance a brief writing sample rather than complete ms is preferred. No reading fee.

Laurence Fitch Ltd

Mezzanine, Quadrant House, 80–82 Regent Street, London W1B 5AU
☎ 020 7734 9911
Email information@laurencefitch.com
Website www.laurencefitch.com

Contact *Brendan Davis*

FOUNDED 1952, incorporating the London Play Company (1922) and in association with Film Rights Ltd (1932). Handles children's and horror books, scripts for theatre, film, TV and radio only. *Commission* UK 10%; Overseas 15%. No unsolicited mss. Send synopsis with sample scene(s) in the first instance. No reading fee.

Fraser Ross Associates

6 Wellington Street, Edinburgh EH6 7EQ
☎ 0131 553 2759/657 4412
Email lindsey.fraser@tiscali.co.uk *and* kjross@tiscali.co.uk

Contact *Lindsey Fraser, Kathryn Ross*

FOUNDED 2002. Handles children's books, adult literary and mainstream fiction. No poetry, short stories, adult fantasy and science fiction, academic, scripts. *Commission* Home 10%; USA & Translation 20%. Unsolicited material welcome; send preliminary letter, first three chapters or equivalent, c.v. and s.a.e. No reading fee.

Futerman, Rose & Associates*

Heston Court Business Estate, 19 Camp Road, London SW19 4UW
☎ 020 8947 0188   Fax 020 8605 2162

Email guy@futermanrose.co.uk
Website www.futermanrose.co.uk

Contact *Guy Rose*

FOUNDED 1984. Handles scripts for film and TV. Commercial fiction and non-fiction with film potential; biography and show business, teenage fiction. No science fiction or fantasy. *Commission* 15–20%. No unsolicited mss. Send preliminary letter with a brief resumé, detailed synopsis and s.a.e.

Annette Green Authors' Agency*

1 East Cliff Road, Tunbridge Wells TN4 9AD
☎ 01892 514275   Fax 01892 518124
Email annettekgreen@aol.com
Website www.annettegreenagency.co.uk

Contact *Address material to the Agency*

FOUNDED 1998. Handles literary and general fiction and non-fiction, popular culture and current affairs, science, music, film, history, biography, children's and teenage fiction. No dramatic scripts or poetry. *Commission* Home 15%; US & Translation 20%. Letter, synopsis, sample chapters and s.a.e. essential. No reading fee.

A.M. Heath & Co. Ltd*

79 St Martin's Lane, London WC2N 4RE
☎ 020 7836 4271   Fax 020 7497 2561
Website www.amheath.com

Contacts *Bill Hamilton, Sara Fisher, Sarah Molloy, Victoria Hobbs*

FOUNDED 1919. Handles fiction, general non-fiction and children's. No dramatic scripts, poetry or short stories. *Commission* Home 10–15%; US & Translation 20%; Film & TV 15%. Preliminary letter and synopsis essential. No reading fee.

David Higham Associates Ltd*

5–8 Lower John Street, Golden Square, London W1F 9HA

☎ 020 7434 5900   Fax 020 7437 1072

Email dha@davidhigham.co.uk

Website www.davidhigham.co.uk

Scripts *Nicky Lund, Georgina Ruffhead, Gemma Hirst*

Books *Anthony Goff, Bruce Hunter, Jacqueline Korn, Veronique Baxter, Caroline Walsh* (children's)

FOUNDED 1935. Handles fiction, general non-fiction (biography, history, current affairs, etc.) and children's books. Also scripts. *Commission* Home 15%; US & Translation 20%. Preliminary letter with synopsis essential in first instance. No reading fee.

Vanessa Holt Ltd*

59 Crescent Road, Leigh-on-Sea SS9 2PF

☎ 01702 473787   Fax 01702 471890

Email vanessa@holtlimited.freeserve.co.uk

Contact *Vanessa Holt*

FOUNDED 1989. Handles general fiction, non-fiction and non-illustrated children's books. No scripts, poetry, academic or technical. Specialises in crime fiction, commercial and literary fiction, and particularly interested in books with potential for sales abroad and/or to TV. *Commission* Home 15%; US & Translation 20%; Radio/TV/Film 15%. No unsolicited mss. Approach by letter in first instance; s.a.e. essential. No reading fee.

The Inspira Group

5 Bradley Road, Enfield EN3 6ES

☎ 020 8292 5163   Fax 0870 139 3057

Email darin@theinspiragroup.com

Website www.theinspiragroup.com

Managing Director *Darin Jewell*

FOUNDED 2001. Handles children's books, fiction, humour, lifestyle/ relationships, science fiction/fantasy. No scripts. *Commission* Home & US 15%. Unsolicited mss and synopses welcome; approach by email or telephone. No reading fee.

International Literary Representation & Management LLC

186 Bickenhall Mansions, Bickenhall Street, London W1U 6BX

☎ 020 7224 1748   Fax 020 7224 1802

Email info@yesitive.com

Website www.yesitive.com

Vice President for Europe *Peter Cox*

European office of US agency. Represents authors with major international potential. *Commission* by agreement. Submissions considered only if the guidelines given on the website have been followed. Do not send unsolicited mss by post. No radio or theatre scripts. No reading fee.

International Literary Rights & Management

18 Mill View Close, Ewell KT17 2DW

☎ 07866 713512

Email MariaWhite2001@aol.com

Contact *Maria White*

FOUNDED 2004. Small agency handling commercial and literary fiction and general non-fiction including history, biography, sports, popular science, popular culture, current affairs, cookery, narrative non-fiction, humour, health, fitness, self-help, mind/body/spirit, children's books. Illustrated and non-illustrated books considered. No science fiction, horror, poetry, short stories or plays. *Commission* Home 15%; US & Translation 20%. Write in first instance with covering letter giving brief c.v., a synopsis and first three chapters together with s.a.e. No disks or email submissions. No reading fee.

Johnson & Alcock*

Clerkenwell House, 45–47 Clerkenwell Green, London EC1R OHT

☎ 020 7251 0125   Fax 020 7251 2172

Email info@johnsonandalcock.co.uk

Contacts *Michael Alcock, Andrew Hewson, Anna Power, Merel Reinink*

FOUNDED 1956. Handles literary and commercial fiction, children's fiction; general non-fiction including current affairs, biography and memoirs, history, lifestyle, health and personal development. No poetry, screenplays, science fiction, technical or academic material. *Commission* Home 15%; US & Translation 20%. No unsolicited mss; approach by letter in the first instance giving details of writing and other media experience, plus synopsis. For fiction send one-page synopsis and first three chapters. S.a.e. essential for response. No reading fee.

Juvenilia

Avington, Near Winchester SO21 1DB

☎ 01962 779656   Fax 01962 779656

Email juvenilia@clara.co.uk

Contact *Rosemary Bromley*

FOUNDED 1973. Handles young/teen fiction and picture books; non-fiction and scripts for TV and radio by existing clients only. No poetry or short stories unless part of a collection or picture book material. *Commission* Home 10%; US 15%; Translation 20%. No unsolicited mss. 'Client list is currently full.' Enquiries by phone, fax or email will not be answered.

LAW*

14 Vernon Street, London W14 ORJ

Email firstname@lawagency.co.uk

Contacts *Mark Lucas, Julian Alexander, Araminta Whitley, Alice Saunders, Celia Hayley, Lucinda Cook, Peta Nightingale, Hannah Bellamy, Philippa Milnes-Smith* (children's), *Helen Mulligan* (children's)

FOUNDED 1996. Handles full-length commercial and literary fiction, non-fiction and children's books. No fantasy (except children's), plays, poetry or textbooks. Film and TV scripts handled for established clients only. *Commission* Home 15%; US & Translation 20%. Unsolicited mss considered; send brief covering letter, short synopsis and two sample chapters. S.a.e. essential. No emailed or disk submissions.

Eunice McMullen Children's Literary Agent Ltd

Low Ibbotsholme Cottage, Off Bridge Lane, Troutbeck Bridge, Windermere LA23 1HU

☎ 01539 448551   Fax 01539 442289

Email eunicemcmullen@totalise.co.uk

Contact *Eunice McMullen*

FOUNDED 1992. Handles all types of children's material in particular picture books. Has 'an excellent' list of picture book authors and illustrators. *Commission* Home 10%; US 15%; Translation 20%. *No unsolicited scripts.* Telephone enquiries only.

Andrew Mann Ltd*

1 Old Compton Street, London W1D 5JA

☎ 020 7734 4751   Fax 020 7287 9264

Email manscript@onetel.net.uk

Contacts *Anne Dewe, Tina Betts, Sacha Elliot*

FOUNDED 1975. Handles fiction, general non-fiction, children's and film, TV, theatre, radio scripts. *Commission* Home 15%; US & Translation 20%. No unsolicited mss. Preliminary letter, synopsis and s.a.e. essential. Email submissions for synopses only. No reading fee.

Sarah Manson Literary Agent

6 Totnes Walk, London N2 0AD

☎ 020 88442 0396

Email info@smliteraryagent.com

Contact *Sarah Manson*

FOUNDED 2002. Handles quality fiction for children and young adults. *Commission* Home 10%; Overseas & Translation 20%. Brief email enquiry or preliminary letter with s.a.e. No reading fee.

Martinez Literary Agency
60 Oakwood Avenue, Southgate, London N14 6QL
☎ 020 8886 5829

Contacts *Mary Martinez, Francoise Budd*

FOUNDED 1988. Handles high-quality fiction, children's books, arts and crafts, interior design, autobiography, biography, popular music, sport and memorabilia books. *Commission* Home 15%; US, Overseas & Translation 20%; Performance Rights 20%. Not accepting any new writers.

Michael Motley Ltd
The Old Vicarage, Tredington, Tewkesbury GL20 7BP
☎ 01684 276390   Fax 01684 297355

Contact *Michael Motley*

FOUNDED 1973. Handles only full-length mss (i.e. 60,000+). No short stories or journalism. No science fiction, horror, poetry or original dramatic material. *Commission* Home 10%; US 15%; Translation 20%. New clients by referral only: no unsolicited material considered. No reading fee.

The Maggie Noach Literary Agency*
22 Dorville Crescent, London W6 0HJ
☎ 020 8748 2926   Fax 020 8748 8057
Email m-noach@dircon.co.uk

Contact *Maggie Noach*

FOUNDED 1982. Pronounced 'no-ack'. Handles a wide range of well-written books including general non-fiction, especially biography, commercial fiction and non-illustrated children's books for ages 7–12. No scientific, academic or specialist non-fiction. No poetry, plays, short stories or books for the very young. Recommended for promising young writers but *very* few new clients taken on as it is considered vital to give individual attention to each author's work. *Commission* Home 15%; US & Translation 20%. Unsolicited mss not welcome. Approach by letter (*not by telephone or email*), giving a brief description of the book and enclosing a few sample pages. Return postage essential. No reading fee.

PFD*

Drury House, 34–43 Russell Street, London WC2B 5HA
☎ 020 7344 1000   Fax 020 7836 9539/7836 9541
Email postmaster@pfd.co.uk
Website www.pfd.co.uk

Joint Chairmen *Anthony Jones, Tim Corrie*
Managing Director *Anthony Baring*
Books *Caroline Dawnay, Michael Sissons, Pat Kavanagh, Charles Walker, Rosemary Canter, Robert Kirby, Simon Trewin, James Gill*
Serial *Pat Kavanagh, Carol MacArthur*
Children's *Rosemary Canter*
Multimedia *Rosemary Scoular*

FOUNDED 1988 as a result of the merger of A. D. Peters & Co. Ltd and Fraser & Dunlop, and was later joined by the June Hall Literary Agency. Handles all sorts of books including fiction and children's, plus scripts for film, theatre, radio and TV material. *Commission* Home 10%; US & Translation 20%. Prospective clients should write 'a full letter, with an account of what he/she has done and wants to do and enclose, when possible, a detailed outline and sample chapters'. Screenplays and TV scripts should be addressed to the 'Film & Script Dept.' Enclose s.a.e. No reading fee. The Children's Dept. accepts unsolicited written material in the form of a covering letter, brief plot summary and one paragraph only of text; submissions from illustrators also welcome.

Pollinger Limited*

9 Staple Inn, London WC1V 7QH

☎ 020 7404 0342   Fax 020 7242 5737

Email info@pollingerltd.com *and* Permissions: permissions@pollingerltd.com

Website www.pollingerltd.com

Chairman *Paul Woolf*
Managing Director *Lesley Pollinger*
Agents *Lesley Pollinger, Joanna Devereux*
Consultants *Leigh Pollinger, Joan Deitch*

FOUNDED 2002. A successor of Laurence Pollinger Limited (founded 1958) and Pearn, Pollinger & Higham. Handles all types of general trade adult and children's fiction and non-fiction books; intellectual property development, illustrators/photographers. *Commission* Home 15%; Translation 20%. Overseas theatrical, and media associates. No unsolicited material.

Rogers, Coleridge & White Ltd*

20 Powis Mews, London W11 1JN

☎ 020 7221 3717   Fax 020 7229 9084

Contacts *Deborah Rogers, Gill Coleridge, Patricia White, Peter Straus, David Miller, Zoe Waldie*

FOUNDED 1967. Handles fiction, non-fiction and children's books. No TV or film scripts, plays or technical books. Rights representative in UK and translation for several New York agents. *Commission* Home 10%; US & Translation 20%. No unsolicited mss, please and no submissions by fax or email.

Uli Rushby-Smith Literary Agency

72 Plimsoll Road, London N4 2EE

☎ 020 7354 2718   Fax 020 7354 2718

Contact *Uli Rushby-Smith*

FOUNDED 1993. Handles fiction and non-fiction, commercial and literary, both adult and children's. Film and TV rights handled in conjunction with a sub-agent. No plays or poetry. *Commission* Home 15%; US & Translation 20%. Represents UK rights for Curtis Brown, New York (children's), 2.13.61 USA, Penguin (Canada), Alice Toledo Agency (NL) and Columbia University Press. Approach with an outline, two or three sample chapters and explanatory letter in the first instance (s.a.e. essential). No disks. No reading fee.

Rosemary Sandberg Ltd

6 Bayley Street, London WC1B 3HB

☎ 020 7304 4110   Fax 020 7304 4109

Email rosemary@sandberg.demon.co.uk

Contact *Rosemary Sandberg*

FOUNDED 1991. In association with Ed Victor Ltd. Specialises in children's writers and illustrators. *Commission* 10%. No unsolicited mss as client list is currently full.

Caroline Sheldon Literary Agency*

Thorley Manor Farm, Thorley, Yarmouth, Isle of Wight PO41 0SJ

☎ 01983 760205

Also at: 71 Hillgate Place, London W8 7SS

Contact *Caroline Sheldon*

FOUNDED 1985. Handles adult fiction, in particular women's, both commercial and literary novels. Also full-length children's fiction. No non-fiction, TV/film scripts unless by book-writing clients. *Commission* Home 10%; US & Translation 20%. Submissions should be sent to Isle of Wight address. Send letter with all relevant details of ambitions and first four chapters of proposed book (enclose large s.a.e.). No reading fee.

Dorie Simmonds Agency*

67 Upper Berkeley Street, London W1H 7QX
☎ 020 7486 9228   Fax 020 7486 8228
Email dhsimmonds@aol.com

Contact *Dorie Simmonds*

Handles a wide range of subjects including general non-fiction and commercial fiction, children's books and associated rights. Specialities include contemporary personalities and historical biographies. *Commission* Home & US 15%; Translation 20%. Outline required for non-fiction; a short synopsis for fiction with 2–3 sample chapters, and a c.v. with writing experience/ publishing history. No reading fee. Return postage essential.

Standen Literary Agency

41b Endymion Road, London N4 1EQ
☎ 020 8245 3053   Fax 020 8245 3053
Email yasmin@standenliteraryagency.com
Website www.standenliteraryagency.com

Contact *Yasmin Standen*

FOUNDED 2004. Handles fiction, both adult and children's. No thrillers, non-fiction, academic. Interested in first time writers. *Commission* Home 15%; Overseas 20%. See website for submissions procedure.

Ed Victor Ltd*

6 Bayley Street, Bedford Square, London WC1B 3HE
☎ 020 7304 4100   Fax 020 7304 4111

Contacts *Ed Victor, Graham Greene, Maggie Phillips, Sophie Hicks, Grainne Fox*

FOUNDED 1976. Handles a broad range of material including children's books but leans towards the more commercial ends of the fiction and non-fiction spectrums. No poetry, scripts or academic. Takes on very few new writers. After trying his hand at book publishing and literary magazines, Ed Victor, an ebullient American, found his true vocation. Strong opinions, very pushy and works hard for those whose intelligence he respects. Loves nothing more than a good title auction. *Commission* Home & US 15%; Translation 20%. No unsolicited mss.

Robin Wade Literary Agency

33 Cormorant Lodge, Thomas More Street, London E1W 1AU
☎ 020 7488 4171   Fax 020 7488 4172
Email rw@rwla.com
Website www.rwla.com

Contact *Robin Wade*
Associate *Jo Kitching*

FOUNDED 2001. Handles general fiction and non-fiction including children's books. No scripts, poetry, plays or short stories. *Commission* Home 10%; Overseas & Translation 20%. 'Fees negotiable if a contract has already been offered.' Send detailed synopsis and two specimen chapters by email with a brief biography. No reading fee.

Cecily Ware Literary Agents

19C John Spencer Square, London N1 2LZ
☎ 020 7359 3787   Fax 020 7226 9828
Email info@cecilyware.com

Contacts *Cecily Ware, Gilly Schuster, Warren Sherman*

FOUNDED 1972. Primarily a film and TV script agency representing work in all areas: drama, children's, series/serials, adaptations, comedies, etc. *Commission* Home 10%; US 10–20% by arrangement. No unsolicited mss or phone calls. Approach in writing only. No reading fee.

Watson, Little Ltd*

Capo Di Monte, Windmill Hill, London NW3 6RJ
☎ 020 7431 0770   Fax 020 7431 7225
Email enquiries@watsonlittle.com

Contacts *Sheila Watson, Mandy Little, Sugra Zaman*

Handles fiction, commercial women's fiction, crime and literary fiction. Non-fiction special interests include history, science, popular psychology, self-help, business and general leisure books. Also children's fiction and non-fiction. No short stories, poetry, TV, play or film scripts. Not interested in purely academic writers. *Commission* Home 15%; US 24%; Translation 19%. No emails or unsolicited mss. Informative preliminary letter and synopsis with return postage essential.

A.P. Watt Ltd*

20 John Street, London WC1N 2DR

☎ 020 7405 6774   Fax 020 7831 2154

Email apw@apwatt.co.uk

Website www.apwatt.co.uk

Directors *Caradoc King, Linda Shaughnessy, Derek Johns, Georgia Garrett, Nick Harris, Natasha Fairweather, Sheila Crowley*

FOUNDED 1875. The oldest-established literary agency in the world. Handles full-length typescripts, including children's books, screenplays for film and TV. No poetry, academic or specialist works. *Commission* Home 10%; US & Translation 20%. No unsolicited mss accepted.

Eve White Literary Agent

Irish Hill House, Hamstead Marshall, Newbury RG20 0JB

☎ 01488 657656

Email evewhite@btinternet.com

Contact *Eve White*

FOUNDED 2003. Handles full-length adult and children's fiction and non-fiction. No poetry, short stories or textbooks. *Commission* Home 15%; US & Translation 20%. No unsolicited mss. Send letter with s.a.e. (include email address and phone number), résumé, synopsis, one-page writing sample. No initial approach by email. No reading fee.

Magazines

Bliss Magazine
Endeavour House, 189 Shaftesbury Avenue, London WC2H 8JG
☎ 020 7208 3478   Fax 020 7208 3591
Email alex.thwaites@emap.com

Owner *Emap élan*
Editor *Helen Johnston*
Circulation 241,664

FOUNDED 1995. MONTHLY teenage lifestyle magazine for girls. No unsolicited mss; 'call the assistant editor (*Chantelle Horton*) with an idea and then send it in.'
NEWS *Charlotte Crisp* Worldwide teenage news. Maximum 200 words.
FEATURES Real life teenage stories with subjects willing to be photographed. Reports on teenage issues. Maximum 2000 words.
PAYMENT news, £50–100; feaures, £350.

Brownie
PO Box 48, Bexley DA5 1WB
☎ 01332 400274   Fax 01332 400274
Email mariontbrownie@aol.com
Website www.girlguiding.org.uk

Owner *The Guide Association*
Editor *Marion Thompson*
Circulation 16,500

FOUNDED 1962. MONTHLY. Aimed at Brownie members aged 7–10.
ARTICLES Crafts and simple make-it-yourself items using inexpensive or scrap materials.
FICTION Brownie content an advantage. No adventures involving unaccompanied children in dangerous situations – day or night. Maximum 650 words. PAYMENT £50 per 1000 words pro rata.

CosmoGIRL!

National Magazine House, 72 Broadwick Street, London W1F 9EP
☎ 020 7439 5000   Fax 020 7439 5400
Email cosmogirl.mail@natmags.co.uk
Website www.cosmogirl.co.uk

Owner *National Magazine Co. Ltd*
Editor *Celia Duncan*
Circulation 198,324

FOUNDED 2001. MONTHLY glossy magazine for 'fun, fearless teens'. Fashion, beauty advice and boys.
FEATURES *Miranda Eason* Interested in ideas – send synopsis by mail – no finished articles.

Dare Magazine

Room A1136, Woodlands, 80 Wood Lane, London W12 0TT

Editor *Mink Kapferer*

FOUNDED 2003. FORTNIGHTLY teen lifestyle magazine: boys, friends, fashion, beauty, celebs, quizzes, cringes, advice and posters. Welcomes real-life and spooky-psychic stories, quizzes. Approach by email (Julie.Bradley@bbc.co.uk).
FEATURES Maximum 900 words.
PAYMENT depends on commission.

It's Hot! Magazine

Rm A1136, BBC Worldwide, Woodlands, 180 Wood Lane, London
W12 0TT

☎ 020 8433 2447   Fax 020 8433 2763

Email itshot@bbc.co.uk

Owner *BBC Worldwide*
Editor *Peter Hart*
Features *Kelly Wilks*
Circulation 116,515

FOUNDED 2002. MONTHLY magazine aimed at celebrity-mad 9–13 year old girls featuring music, film & TV gossip. Interested in exclusive celebrity interviews relevant to their market, and quizzes. Approach the editor with ideas by Email (peter.hart@bbc.co.uk) but 'please read the magazine first for style'. PAYMENT negotiable.

Mizz

IPC Media Ltd., King's Reach Tower, Stamford Street, London
SE1 9LS

☎ 020 7261 6319   Fax 020 7261 6032

Owner *IPC Media*
Editor *Sharon Christal*
Deputy Editor *Leslie Sinoway*
Circulation 100,298

FOUNDED 1985. FORTNIGHTLY magazine for the 10–14-year-old girl. FEATURES 'We have a full features team and thus do not accept freelance features.'

Sneak Magazine

Mappin House, 4 Winsley Street, London W1W 8HF

☎ 020 7436 1515   Fax 020 7312 8229

Email michelle.garnett@emap.com

Website www.sneakmagazine.com

Owner *EMAP*
Editor *Michelle Garnett*
Editorial Director *Jennifer Cawthron*
Circulation 104,174

FOUNDED 2002. WEEKLY magazine for teenagers providing gossip and entertainment. Unsolicited material welcome.
FEATURES *Leo Roberts*
NEWS *Kate Taylor*
FICTION *Louise Christie.* Approach by email.

Sugar Magazine
64 North Row, London W1K 7LL
☎ 020 7150 7050   Fax 020 7150 7678

Owner *Hachette Filipacchi (UK)*
Editor *Nick Chalmers*
Editorial Director *Lysanne Currie*
Circulation 291,794

FOUNDED 1994. MONTHLY. Everything that might interest the teenage girl. No unsolicited mss. Will consider ideas or contacts for real-life features. No fiction. Approach in writing in the first instance.

Top of the Pops Magazine
Room A1136, Woodlands, 80 Wood Lane, London W12 0TT
☎ 020 8433 3910   Fax 020 8433 2694
Website www.beeb.com/totp

Owner *BBC Worldwide Publishing Ltd*
Editor *Corinna Shaffer*
Circulation 230,493

FOUNDED 1995. MONTHLY teenage pop music magazine with a lighthearted and humorous approach. No unsolicited material apart from pop star interviews.

Young Voices

Voice Group Limited, Blue Star House, 234–244 Stockwell Road, London sw9 9UG

☎ 020 7737 7377   Fax 020 7274 8894

Website www.young-voices.co.uk

Managing Director *Linda McCalla*
Group Editor *Deidre Forbes*
Editor *Emelia Kenlock*

FOUNDED 2003. MONTHLY glossy magazine aimed at 11–19-year-olds. 'Provides a new outlet for today's youth.' Latest news features, showbiz insight and reviews. Also covers current affairs topics that affect readers' lives.

Young Writer

Glebe House, Weobley, Hereford HR4 8SD

☎ 01544 318901   Fax 01544 318901

Email editor@youngwriter.org

Website www.youngwriter.org

Editor *Kate Jones*

Describing itself as 'The Magazine for Children with Something to Say', *Young Writer* is issued three times a year, at the back-to-school times of September, January and April. A forum for young people's writing – fiction and non-fiction, prose and poetry – the magazine is an introduction to independent writing for young writers aged 5–18. PAYMENT from £20 to £100 for freelance commissioned articles (these can be from adult writers).

BBC TV and Radio

Drama, Entertainment and Children's Division

Director *Alan Yentob*

BBC *writersroom* champions writers across all BBC platforms, running targeted schemes and workshops linked directly to production. It accepts, and assesses unsolicited scripts for film, single TV dramas, comedy and radio drama. Produces a Website www.bbc.co.uk/writersroom with diary of events, opportunities and competitions, interviews with established writers, submission guidelines, free formatting software and a lively messageboard. Also runs *northern exposure* which focuses on new writing in the north of England, channelled through theatres in Liverpool, Manchester, Bradford, Leeds and Newcastle. To be considered for one of the schemes run by *writersroom*, send a sample full length drama script to: BBC *writersroom*, 1 Mortimer Street, London w1T 3JA. For guidelines on unsolicited scripts please log on to the website or send a large s.a.e. to *Jessica Dromgoole*, New Writing Coordinator, BBC Drama, Entertainment and CBBC at the Mortimer Street address above. For details of TV and Radio Commissioning log on to www.bbc.co.uk/commissioning

Drama
Controller, Drama Commissioning *Jane Tranter*
Controller, Continuing Drama Series *Mal Young*
Head of Drama Commissioning *Gareth Neame*

Head of Drama Serials *Laura Mackie*
Head of Development, Drama Series *Sarah Cullen*
Controller, Daytime Drama, Factual Entertainment & Entertainment on BBC One/Two: *Alison Sharman* (daytime.proposals@bbc.co.uk)
Head of Films *David Thompson*
Head of Development, Films *Tracey Scoffield*
Creative Director, New Writing *Kate Rowland*
Head of Radio Drama *Gordon House*
Executive Producer (Birmingham)/Editor, The Archers *Vanessa Whitburn*
Executive Producer (World Service Drama) *Marion Nancarrow*

ENTERTAINMENT
Controller, Entertainment Commissioning *Jane Lush*
Head of Comedy Entertainment, Television *Jon Plowman*
Head of Comedy Commissioning *Mark Freeland*
Producer *Bill Dare*
Head of Light Entertainment, Radio 4 *John Pidgeon*
Get Writing: www.bbc.co.uk/dna/getwriting/ is BBC Learning's new service which aims 'to help people get back into or start out in creative writing'.
Programmes produced range from *The Kumars at No 42* and *The Weakest Link* on television to *Loose Ends* and *The Now Show* on Radio 4. Virtually every comic talent in Britain got their first break writing one-liners for topical comedy weeklies.

CBBC (CHILDREN'S)
Controller, CBBC *Dorothy Prior*
Head of Production *Karen Woodward*
Head of Acquisitions *Michael Carrington*
Head of CBBC Drama *Elaine Sperber*
Head of Entertainment *Anne Gilchrist*
Head of CBBC News and Factual Programmes *Roy Milani*
Head of CBBC Pre-school *Clare Elstow*
Head of CBBC Education *Sue Nott*

Film, TV and Radio Production Companies

The Children's Film & Television Foundation Ltd

The John Maxwell Building, Elstree Film & TV Studios, Shenley Road, Borehamwood WD6 1JG

☎ 020 8953 0844   Fax 020 8207 0860

Email annahome@cftf.onyxnet.co.uk

Chief Executive *Anna Home*

Involved in the development and co-production of films for children and the family, both for the theatric market and for TV.

Collingwood & Convergence Productions Ltd

10–14 Crown Street, London W3 8SB

☎ 020 8993 3666   Fax 020 8993 9595

Email info@crownstreet.co.uk

Producers *Christopher O'Hare, Terence Clegg, Tony Collingwood*
Head of Development *Helen Stroud*

Film and TV. Convergence Productions produces live action, drama documentaries; Collingwood O'Hare Entertainment specialises in children's animation. Output **Convergence**: *Theo* (film drama series); *Plastic Fantastic* (UK cosmetic surgery techniques, Ch5); *David Starkey's Henry VIII* (Ch4 historical documentary) and *On the Road Again* (BBC2 documentary travel series). **Collingwood**: *RARG* (award-winning animated film); *Captain Zed and the Zee Zone* (ITV); *Daisy-Head Mayzie* (Dr Seuss animated series for Turner Network and Hanna-Barbera); *Animal Stories* (animated poems, ITV network); *Eddy and the Bear* (CITV) and *The King's Beard* (CITV). Unsolicited mss not welcome 'as a general rule as we do not have the capacity to process the sheer weight of submissions this creates. We therefore tend to review material from individuals recommended to us through personal contact with agents or other industry professionals. We like to encourage new writing and have worked with new writers but our ability to do so is limited by our capacity for development. We can usually only consider taking on one project each year, as development/finance takes several years to put in place.'

The Comedy Unit

Glasgow TV & Film Studios, Glasgow Media Park, Craigmont Street, Glasgow G20 9BT

☎ 0141 305 6666   Fax 0141 305 6600

Email comedyunit@comedyunit.co.uk

Website www.comedyunit.co.uk

Contacts *April Chamberlain, Colin Gilbert*

Producers of comedy entertainment for children's TV, radio, video and film. Output *Still Game; Karen Dunbar Show; Offside; Chewin' the Fat; Only An Excuse; Yo! Diary* and *Watson's Wind Up*. Unsolicited mss welcome by post or email.

Cosgrove Hall Films

8 Albany Road, Chorlton – cum – Hardy M21 0AW

☎ 0161 882 2500   Fax 0161 882 2555

Email animation@chf.co.uk

Contact *Lee Marriott*

Children's animation producer; film video and television. OUTPUT includes *Noddy* and *Rotten Ralph* (both for BBC); *Lavender Castle* by Gerry Anderson;

The Fox Busters; Animal Shelf; Rocky & the Dodos; Alison Uttley's *Little Grey Rabbit* (all for children's ITV); Terry Pratchett's *Discworld* (Ch4). 'We try to select writers on a project-by-project basis.'

Farnham Film Company Ltd
34 Burnt Hill Road, Lower Bourne, Farnham GU10 3LZ
☎ 01252 710313   Fax 01252 725855
Website www.farnfilm.com

Contact *Ian Lewis*

Television and film: children's drama and documentaries. Unsolicited mss usually welcome but prefers a letter to be sent in the first instance. Check website for current requirements.

Festival Film and Television Ltd
Festival House, Tranquil Passage, Blackheath, London SE3 0BJ
☎ 020 8297 9999   Fax 020 8297 1155
Email info@festivalfilm.com

Contacts *Ray Marshall, Matt Marshall*

Specialises in television drama. In the last ten years has produced the Catherine Cookson drama for ITV. Now made its first feature film *Man Dancin'*. Looking primarily for commercial projects for both cinema and TV. Features: should be 'feel good'/family or projects with 'heart'. No horror or violence. TV: mainly looking for series or 2/3 parters. Not particularly interested in 'period'. Prefers submissions through an agent. Unsolicited work must be professionally presented or it will be returned unread.

Flicks Films Ltd
101 Wardour Street, London W1F 0UG
☎ 020 7734 4892   Fax 020 7287 2307
Website www.flicksfilms.com

Managing Director/Producer *Terry Ward*

Film and video: children's animated series and specials. Output *The Mr Men; Little Miss; Bananaman; The Pondles; Nellie the Elephant; See How They Work With Dig and Dug; Timbuctoo.* Scripts specific to their needs will be considered. 'Always willing to read relevant material.'

Sianco Cyf

36 Y Maes, Caernarfon LL55 2NN
☎ 01286 676100/07831 726111 (Mobile)   Fax 01286 677616
Email post@sianco.tv

Contact *Siân Teifi*

Children's, youth and education programmes, children's drama, people-based documentaries for adults.

Siriol Productions

3 Mount Stuart Square, Butetown, Cardiff CF10 5EE
☎ 029 2048 8400   Fax 029 2048 5962
Email enquiries@siriol.co.uk
Website www.siriolproductions.com

Contact *Andrew Offiler*

Animated series, mainly for children. Output includes *Meeow; Hilltop Hospital; The Hurricanes; Tales of the Toothfairies; Billy the Cat; The Blobs,* as well as the feature films, *Under Milkwood* and *The Princess and the Goblin.* Write with ideas and sample script in the first instance.

SMG & Ginger TV Productions Ltd

SMG: 200 Renfield Street, Glasgow G2 3PR
☎ 0141 300 3000
Ginger TV Productions: 116 New Oxford Street, London WC1A 1HH
☎ 020 7663 2300
Website www.ginger.com

Managing Director (SMG) *Elizabeth Partyka*
Head of Drama *Eric Coulter*
Head of Factual Programming *Helen Alexander*

SMG (Scottish Media Group) TV Productions Ltd, which incorporates Ginger Television, makes programmes for the national television networks, including ITV, Ch4 and Sky. Specialises in drama, factual entertainment and children's programming.

Sunset + Vine Productions Ltd

30 Sackville Street, London W1S 3DY
☎ 020 7478 7300   Fax 020 7478 7403

Sports, children's and music programmes for television. No unsolicited mss. 'We hire freelancers only upon receipt of a commission.'

Brian Waddell Productions Ltd

Strand Studios, 5/7 Shore Road, Holywood BT18 9HX
☎ 028 9042 7646   Fax 028 9042 7922
Email strand@bwpltv.co.uk

Contacts *Brian Waddell*

Producer of a wide range of television programmes in leisure activities, the arts, children's, travel/adventure and documentaries.

Working Title Films Ltd

Oxford House, 76 Oxford Street, London W1D 1BS
☎ 020 7307 3000   Fax 020 7307 3001/2/3

Co-Chairmen (Films) *Tim Bevan, Eric Fellner*
Head of Development (Films) *Debra Hayward*
Development Coordinator *Luke Parker Bowles*
Television *Simon Wright*

Feature films, TV drama; also family/children's entertainment and TV comedy. Output Films: *Love Actually; Thunderbirds; Ned Kelly; Johnny English;*

Bridget Jones's Diary; Captain Corelli's Mandolin; Ali G in da House; Notting Hill; Elizabeth; Plunkett & Macleane; The Borrowers; The Matchmaker; Fargo; Dead Man Walking; French Kiss; Four Weddings and a Funeral; The Hudsucker Proxy; The Tall Guy; Wish You Were Here; My Beautiful Laundrette. Television: *More Tales of the City; The Borrowers I & II; Armisted Maupin's Tales of the City; News Hounds; Randall & Hopkirk Deceased; Doomwatch.* No unsolicited mss at present.

Theatre Producers

Graeae Theatre Company
LVS Resource Centre, 356 Holloway Road, London N7 6PA
☎ 020 7700 2455   Fax 020 7609 7324
Email info@graeae.org
Website www.graeae.org

Minicom 020 7700 8184
Artistic Director *Jenny Sealey*
Executive Producer *Roger Nelson*

Europe's premier theatre company of disabled people, the company tours nationally and internationally with innovative theatre productions highlighting both historical and contemporary disabled experience. Graeae also runs Forum Theatre and educational programmes available to schools, youth clubs and day centres nationally, provides vocational training in theatre arts (including playwriting). Unsolicited scripts, from disabled writers, welcome. New work is commissioned.

The Hiss & Boo Company Ltd
1 Nyes Hill, Wineham Lane, Bolney RH17 5SD   Fax 01444 882057
Email hissboo@msn.com
Website www.hissboo.co.uk

Contact *Ian Liston*

Particularly interested in new thrillers, comedy thrillers, comedy and melodrama – must be commercial full-length plays. Also interested in plays/plays with music for children. No one-acts. Previous productions: *The Shakespeare Revue; Come Rain Come Shine; Sleighrider; Beauty and the Beast; An Ideal Husband; Mr Men's Magical Island; Mr Men and the Space Pirates; Nunsense; Corpse!; Groucho: A Life in Revue; See How They Run; Christmas Cat and the Pudding Pirates; Pinocchio* and traditional pantos written by Roy Hudd for the company. 'We are keen on revue-type shows and compilation shows but *not* tribute-type performances.' No unsolicited scripts; no telephone calls. Send synopsis and introductory letter in the first instance.

Norwich Puppet Theatre
St James, Whitefriars, Norwich NR3 1TN
☎ 01603 615564   Fax 01603 617578
Email norpuppet@hotmail.com
Website www.puppettheatre.co.uk

Artistic Director *Luis Boy*
General Manager *Ian Woods*

Plays to a young audience (aged 3–12) but developing shows for adult audiences interested in puppetry. All year round programme plus tours to schools and arts venues. Most productions are based on traditional stories but unsolicited mss welcome if relevant.

Nottingham Playhouse Roundabout Theatre in Education
Wellington Circus, Nottingham NG1 5AF
☎ 0115 947 4361   Fax 0115 953 9055
Email andrewb@nottinghamplayhouse.co.uk
Website www.nottinghamplayhouse.co.uk

Contact *Andrew Breakwell*

FOUNDED 1973. Theatre-in-Education company of the **Nottingham Playhouse**. Plays to a young audience aged 5–18 years of age. 'Most of our current work uses existing scripts but we try and commission at least one new play every year. We are committed to the encouragement of new writing as and when resources permit. With other major producers in the East Midlands we share the resources of the *Theatre Writing Partnership* which is based at the Playhouse. See website for philosophy and play details. Please make contact before submitting scripts.'

Polka Theatre for Children

240 The Broadway, Wimbledon SW19 1SB
☎ 020 8545 8320   Fax 020 8545 8365
Email info@polkatheatre.com
Website www.polkatheatre.com

Artistic Director *Annie Wood*
Executive Director *Stephen Midlane*
Director of New Writing *Richard Shannon*

FOUNDED in 1967 and moved into its Wimbledon base in 1979. Leading children's theatre committed to commissioning and producing new plays. Programmes are planned two years ahead and at least three new plays are commissioned each year. 'Many of our scripts are commissioned from established writers. We are, however, keen to develop work from writers new to children and young people's theatre. We run a new writing programme which includes master classes and workshops. Potential new writers' work is read and discussed on a regular basis; thus we constantly add to our pool of interesting and interested writers. This department is now headed by a new position, Director of New Writing.'

Snap People's Theatre Trust

29 Raynham Road, Bishop's Stortford CM23 5PE
☎ 01279 461607   Fax 01279 506694

Email info@snaptheatre.co.uk
Website www.snaptheatre.co.uk

Contacts *Andy Graham, Gill Bloomfield*

FOUNDED 1979. Plays to young people (5–11; 12–19), and for the under 25s. New writing, young people and new media are the priorities. Writers should make contact in advance of sending material. New writing is encouraged and should involve, be written for or by young people. 'Projects should reflect the writer's own beliefs, be thought-provoking, challenging and accessible. The writer should be able to work with designers, directors and musicians in the early stages to develop the text and work alongside other disciplines.'

Theatre Workshop Edinburgh

34 Hamilton Place, Edinburgh EH3 5AX
☎ 0131 225 7942   Fax 0131 220 0112

Artistic Director *Robert Rae*

First ever professional producing theatre to fully include disabled actors in all its productions. Plays to a young, broad-based audience with many pieces targeted towards particular groups or communities. Output has included *D.A.R.E.* Particularly interested in issues-based work for young people and minority groups. Frequently engages writers for collaborative work and devised projects. Commissions a significant amount of new writing for a wide range of contexts, from large-scale community plays to small-scale professional productions. Favours writers based in Scotland, producing material relevant to a contemporary Scottish audience.

Tiebreak Theatre Company

42–58 St George's Street, Norwich NR3 1AB
☎ 01603 665899   Fax 01603 666096
Email info@tiebreak-theatre.com
Website www.tiebreak-theatre.com

Artistic Director David Farmer

FOUNDED 1981. Specialises in high-quality theatre for children and young people, touring schools, youth centres, small-scale theatres, museums and festivals. Productions: *Frog in Love; My Uncle Arly; Time and Tide; The Snow Egg; One Dark Night; Suitcase Full of Stories; Fast Eddy; Breaking the Rules; George Speaks; Frog and Toad; Singing in the Rainforest; The Invisible Boy; My Friend Willy; The Ugly Duckling.* New writing encouraged. Interested in low-budget, small-cast material only. School and educational material of special interest. 'Scripts welcome but please ring first to discuss any potential submission.'

Unicorn Theatre for Children

St Mark's Studios, Chillingworth Road, London N7 8QJ
☎ 020 7700 0702   Fax 020 7700 3870
Email admin@unicorntheatre.com
Website www.unicorntheatre.com

Artistic Director *Tony Graham*
Literary Manager *Carl Miller*

FOUNDED 1947, resident at the Arts Theatre from 1967 to 1999. Produces full-length professionally performed plays for children, aged 4–12, their teachers and families. Recent work includes *Clockwork* by Philip Pullman, adapt. David Wood and Stephen McNeff; *Rumpelstiltskin* by Mike Kenny; *Merlin the Magnificent* by Stuart Paterson; *Great Expectations* by Charles Dickens, adapted by John Clifford. Currently produces at London venues including the Pleasance Theatre, Royal Opera House, the Linbury Theatre and on tour nationally and internationally. Moving to new Unicorn Children's Centre with two theatres on Bankside, London, in 2005. Does not produce unsolicited scripts but works with commissioned writers. Writers interested in working with the company should send details of relevant previous work and why they would like to write for Unicorn.

Whirligig Theatre

14 Belvedere Drive, Wimbledon, London sw19 7BY

☎ 020 8947 1732   Fax 020 8879 7648

Email whirligig-theatre@virgin.net

Contact *David Wood*

Occasional productions and tours to major theatre venues, usually a musical for primary school audiences and weekend family groups. Interested in scripts which exploit the theatrical nature of children's tastes. Previous productions: *The See-Saw Tree*; *The Selfish Shellfish*; *The Gingerbread Man*; *The Old Man of Lochnagar*; *The Ideal Gnome Expedition*; *Save the Human*; *Dreams of Anne Frank*; *Babe, the Sheep-Pig*.

Festivals

Northern Children's Book Festival
Schools Library Service, Sandhill Centre, Grindon Lane,
Sunderland SR3 4EN
☎0191553 8866/7/8   Fax 0191 553 8869
Email schools.library@sunderland.gov.uk
Website www.ncbf.org.uk

Secretary *Eleanor Dowley*

FOUNDED 1984. Annual two-week festival during November. Events in
schools and libraries for children in the North East region. One Saturday
during the festival sees the staging of a large book event hosted by one of
the local authorities involved.

Royal Festival Hall Literature & Talks
Performing Arts Department, Royal Festival Hall, London SE1 8XX
☎020 7921 0906   Fax 020 7928 2049
Email awhitehead@rfh.org.uk
Website www.sbc.org.uk

Head of Literature & Talks *Ruth Borthwick*

The Royal Festival Hall presents a year-round literature programme
covering all aspects of writing. Regular series range from A Life Indeed!

to Fiction International and there are two biennial festivals: Poetry International and Imagine: Writers and Writing for Children. Literature events are now programmed in the Voice Box, Purcell Room and Queen Elizabeth Hall. To join the free mailing list, call 020 7921 0971 or email Literature&Talks@rfh.org.uk

The Scottish Book Town Festival

Wigtown Book Town Company, County Buildings, Wigtown DG8 9JH

☎ 01988 402036   Fax 01988 402506

Email info@wigtown-booktown.co.uk

Website www.wigtown-booktown.co.uk

Contact *Jennifer Bradley*

FOUNDED 1999. A rural literary festival which takes place annually at the end of September in Wigtown town centre, many of the town's bookshops and the nearby Bladnoch Distillery. Authors' readings, including children's authors, debates, poetry, music and film.

Professional Associations

Booktrust

Book House, 45 East Hill, London SW18 2QZ

☎ 020 8516 2977   Fax 020 8516 2978

Email info@booktrust.org.uk

Website www.booktrust.org.uk *and* www.booktrusted.com

Director *Chris Meade*
Press & Publicity *Helen Hayes*

FOUNDED 1925. Booktrust, the independent educational charity promoting books and reading, runs the Book Information Line giving accurate facts about topical books and the book world (☎ 0906 516 1193, weekdays 10 am to 1.00 pm; calls charged at £1.50 per minute). Runs Booktrusted.com, their website for all those who care what young people read which includes details of Children's Book Week and Booktrusted publications. Administers many literary prizes such as the Orange Prize and creative reading projects like Bookscapes, and runs Bookstart, the acclaimed national scheme which aims to supply a free introductory bag of baby books to all babies at their eight-month health check. Booktrust recently launched the Booktrust Teen-age Prize for fiction only.

Children's Book Circle

c/o Egmont Books Ltd, 239 Kensington High Street, London W8 6SA

Email nwilkinson@euk.egmont.com
Website www.childrensbookcircle.org.uk

Membership Secretary *Nicola Wilkinson*

The Children's Book Circle provides a discussion forum for anybody involved with children's books. Regular meetings are addressed by a panel of invited speakers and topics focus on current and controversial issues. Administers the Eleanor Farjeon Award.

Children's Books Ireland

17 Lower Camden Street, Dublin 2, Republic of Ireland
☎ 00 353 1 872 5854   Fax 00 353 1 872 5854
Email info@childrensbooksireland.com
Website www.childrensbooksireland.com

Contact *Claire Ranson*
SUBSCRIPTION £25 p.a. (Individual); £35 (Institutions); £15 (Students); £45/ US$40 (Overseas)

Aims to promote quality children's books and reading. Holds annual spring seminar, summer school and autumn conference for adults. Quarterly magazine, *Inis* and bi-monthly newsletter, *Children's Book News*. Annual children's book festival in October; Bisto/CBI Book of the Year Award. Publishes *Book Choice for Primary Schools; Book Choice for Post Primary Schools; The Big Guide 2: Irish Children's Books, What's The Story? The Reading Choices of Young People in Ireland* .

Scottish Book Trust

Sandeman House, Trunk's Close, 55 High Street, Edinburgh EH1 1SR
☎ 0131 524 0161   Fax 0131 524 0160
Email info@scottishbooktrust.com
Website www.scottishbooktrust.com

Contact *Mark Lambert*

FOUNDED 1956. Scottish Book Trust exists to serve readers and writers in Scotland. 'We work to ensure that everyone has access to good books and to related resources and opportunities. We do this by operating the 'Live Literature Scotland' which funds over 1400 visits a year by Scottish writers to a variety of institutions and groups; by supporting Scottish writing through a programme of professional training opportunities for writers; by publishing a wide variety of resources and leaflets to support readership; by promoting initiatives such as National Poetry Day and World Book Day; through our Book Information Service providing free advice and support to readers and writers and the general public.'

Society for Children's Book Writers & Illustrators
Flat 3, 124 Norwood Road, London SE24 9AY
Email scbwi_bi@hotmail.com
Website www.wordpool.co.uk/scbwi

British Isles Regional Advisor *Natascha Biebow*

FOUNDED in 1968 by a group of Los Angeles-based writers, the SCBWI is the only international professional organisation for the exchange of information between writers, illustrators, editors, publishers, agents and others involved with literature for young people. With a membership of 18,000 worldwide, it holds three annual international conferences plus a number of regional events, publishes a bi-monthly newsletter and awards grants for works in progress. The British Isles region meets quarterly for speaker events and holds an Illustrator's Day in the spring and a Writer's Day in the autumn. It facilitates critique groups and publishes a quarterly regional newsletter. For membership enquiries, contact the address above.

Literary Societies

The Children's Books History Society
25 Field Way, Hoddesdon EN11 0QN
☎ 01992 464775
Email cbhs@abcgarrett.demon.co.uk
Chair/Membership Secretary *Mrs Pat Garrett*
SUBSCRIPTIONS £10 p.a. (UK/Europe); writer for overseas subscription details

Established 1969. Aims to promote an appreciation of children's books and to study their history, bibliography and literary content. The Society holds approximately six meetings per year in London and a summer meeting to a collection, or to a location with a children's book connection. Three substantial newsletters issued annually, with an occasional paper. Review copies should be sent to Newsletter co-editor Mrs Pat Garrett (address above). The Society constitutes the British branch of the Friends of the Osborne and Lillian H. Smith Collections in Toronto, Canada, and also liaises with CILIP (formerly The Library Association). In 1990, the Society established its biennial Harvey Darton Award for a book, published in English, which extends our knowledge of some aspect of British children's literature of the past.

Folly (Fans of Light Literature for the Young)

21 Warwick Road, Pokesdown, Bournemouth BH7 6JW

☎ 01202 432562   Fax 01202 460059

Email folly@sims.abel.co.uk

Contact *Mrs Sue Sims*

SUBSCRIPTIONS £9 p.a. (UK); £11 (Europe); £14 (Worldwide)

FOUNDED 1990 to promote interest in a wide variety of children's authors – with a bias towards writers of girls' books and school stories. Publishes three magazines a year.

Violet Needham Society

c/o 19 Ashburnham Place, London SE10 8TZ

☎ 020 8692 4562

Email richardcheffins@aol.com

Honorary Secretary *R.H.A. Cheffins*

SUBSCRIPTIONS £7.50 p.a. (UK & Europe); £11 (RoW)

FOUNDED 1985 to celebrate the work of children's author Violet Needham and stimulate critical awareness of her work. Publishes thrice-yearly *Souvenir*, the Society journal with an accompanying newsletter; organises meetings and excursions to places associated with the author and her books. The journal includes articles about other children's writers of the 1940s and '50s and on ruritanian fiction. Contributions welcome.

The Edith Nesbit Society

21 Churchfields, West Malling ME19 6RJ

Website www.imagix.dial.pipex.com

Chairman *Margaret McCarthy*

SUBSCRIPTIONS £6 p.a.; £8 (Joint); £75 (Life)

FOUNDED in 1996 to celebrate the life and work of Edith Nesbit (1858–1924), best known as the author of *The Railway Children*. The Society's activities include a regular newsletter, booklets, talks and visits to relevant places.

The Malcolm Saville Society

78a Windmill Road, Mortimer RG7 3RL
Email mystery@witchend.com
Website www.witchend.com

Membership Secretary *Richard Griffiths*
SUBSCRIPTIONS £7.50 p.a. (UK); £12 (Overseas)

FOUNDED in 1994 to remember and promote interest in the work of the popular children's author. Regular social activities, booksearch, library, contact directory and four magazines per year.

Arts Councils and Regional Offices

The Arts Council England

14 Great Peter Street, London SW1P 3NQ

☎ 020 7333 0100   Fax 020 7973 6564 Textphone 020 7973 6564

Email enquiries@artscouncil.org.uk

Website www.artscouncil.org.uk

Chairman *Professor Sir Christopher Frayling*
Chief Executive *Peter Hewitt*
Director of Literature *Gary McKeone*

Arts Council England is the national development agency for the arts in England, distributing public money from government and the National Lottery to artists and arts organisations. Arts Council England works independently and at arm's length from government. Information about Arts Council England funding is available on the website, by Email or by contacting the enquiry line on 0845 300 6200.

Arts Council England has 9 regional offices:

Arts Council England, East

Eden House, 48–49 Bateman Street, Cambridge CB2 1LR

☎ 0845 300 6200   Fax 0870 242 1271 Textphone 01223 306893

Arts Council England, East Midlands
St Nicholas Court, 25–27 Castle Gate, Nottingham NG1 7AR
☎ 0845 300 6200   Fax 0115 950 2467

Arts Council England, London
2 Pear Tree Court, London EC1R 0DS
☎ 0845 300 6200   Fax 020 7608 4100 Textphone 020 7608 4101
Head of Literature *Nick McDowell*

Arts Council England, North East
Central Square, Forth Street, Newcastle upon Tyne NE1 3PJ
☎ 0845 300 6200   Fax 0191 230 1020 Textphone 0191 255 8500

Arts Council England, North West
Manchester House, 22 Bridge Street Manchester M3 3AB
☎ 0161 834 6644   Fax 0161 834 6969 Textphone 0161 834 9131

Arts Council England, South East
Sovereign House, Church Street, Brighton BN1 1RA
☎ 0845 300 6200   Fax 0870 242 1257 Textphone 01273 710659

Arts Council England, South West
Bradninch Place, Gandy Street, Exeter EX4 3LS
Tel 0845 300 6200   Fax 01392 229229 Textphone 01392 433503

Arts Council England, West Midlands
82 Granville Street, Birmingham B1 2LH
☎ 0845 300 6200   Fax 0121 643 7239 Textphone 0121 643 2815

Arts Council England, Yorkshire
21 Bond Street, Dewsbury WF13 1AX
☎ 0845 300 6200   Fax 01924 466522 Textphone 01924 438585

The Arts Council/An Chomhairle Ealaíon
70 Merrion Square, Dublin 2 Republic of Ireland
☎ 00 353 1 618 0200   Fax 00 353 1 676 1302
Email artistsservices@artscouncil.ie
Website www.artscouncil.ie

Director *Patricia Quinn*
Literature Specialist (English language) *Bronwen Williams*
Literature Specialist (Irish language) *Róisin Ní Mhianáin*
Artists' Services Manager *Paul Johnson*

The development agency for the arts in Ireland. An autonomous statutory body, appointed by the Irish government to promote and assist the arts. Established by the Arts Act of 1951. In fulfilling its remit, the Council provides advice to the Irish government on artistic matters; advice, assistance and support to individuals, arts organisations and a wide range of governmental and non-governmental bodies; and financial assistance to individuals and organisations for artistic purposes. The Council also part funds county and city arts officers throughout the country. It consists of 12 members and a chair appointed by the Minister for Arts, Sport and Tourism for a period of not more than five years. Its state grant in 2004 was £52.5 million.

Of particular interest to individual writes is the Council's free booklet, *Support for Artists*, which describes bursaries, awards and schemes on offer and how to apply for them. Applicants to these awards must be of Irish birth or resident in Ireland.

The Arts Council of Northern Ireland
MacNeice House, 77 Malone Road, Belfast BT9 6AQ
☎ 028 9038 5200   Fax 028 9066 1715
Email rmeredith@artscouncil-ni.org
Website www.artscouncil-ni.org

Literature and Language Arts Officer *Robbie Meredith*

Funds book production by established publishers, programmes of readings, literary festivals, writers-in-residence schemes and literary magazines and periodicals. Occasional schools programmes and anthologies of children's writing are produced. Annual awards and bursaries for writers are available. Holds information also on various groups associated with local arts, workshops and courses.

Scottish Arts Council

12 Manor Place, Edinburgh EH3 7DD
☎ 0131 226 6051   Fax 0131 225 9833
Email administrator@scottisharts.org.uk
Website www.scottisharts.org.uk

Chairman *James Boyle*
Director *Graham Berry*
Head of Literature *Gavin Wallace*
Literature Officers *Jenny Attala, Sophy Dale*
Literature Secretary *Catherine Allen*

Principal channel for government funding of the arts in Scotland. The Scottish Arts Council (SAC) is funded by the Scottish Executive. It aims to develop and improve the knowledge, understanding and practice of the arts, and to increase their accessibility throughout Scotland. It offers around 1300 grants a year to artists and arts organisations concerned with the visual arts, crafts dance and mime, drama, literature, music, festivals and traditional, ethnic and community arts. It is also a distributor of National Lottery funds to the arts in Scotland. SAC's support for Scottish-based writers with a track record of publication includes bursaries, writing fellowships and book awards. Information offered includes lists of literature awards, literary magazines, agents and publishers.

The Arts Council of Wales

Museum Place, Cardiff CF10 3NX
☎ 029 2037 6500   Fax 029 2022 1447
Website www.artswales.org

Senior Officer: Drama *Sandra Wynne*

In April 2003 the responsibility for funding literary magazines and book production transferred to the Welsh Books Council. Services for individual writers including bursaries, mentoring, the critical writers service and writers in residency/writers on tour are provided by the Welsh Academy, Hay-on-Wye Literature Festival and Ty Newydd Writers' Centre at Cricieth. The Council aims to develop theatrical experience among Wales-based writers through a variety of schemes – in particular, by funding writers on year-long attachments.

Writers' Courses

England

Buckinghamshire

Missenden Abbey Adult Learning
Great Missenden HP16 0BD
☎ 0845 045 4040   Fax 01753 783756
Email adultlearningchil@buckscc.gov.uk
Website www.aredu.org.uk/missendenabbey

Residential and non-residential weekend workshops, Easter and summer school. Programmes have included *Writing Stories for Children; Short Story Writing; Poetry Workshop; Writing for TV and Film; Writing Comedy for Television; Life Writing; Travel Tales.*

Derbyshire

University of Derby
Student Information Centre, Kedleston Road, Derby DE22 1GB
☎ 01332 622236   Fax 01332 622754
Email J.Bains@derby.ac.uk (prospectus requests only)
Website www.derby.ac.uk
Contact *Graham Parker*

With upwards of 300 students, *Creative Writing* runs 21 modules as part of the undergraduate degree programme, including *Storytelling; Poetry; Playwriting; Writing for TV and Radio; The Short Story; Journalism; Writing for Children*. The courses are all led by practising writers.

Hampshire

King Alfred's College
Winchester SO22 4NR
☎ 01962 841515   Fax 01962 842280
Website www.kingalfreds.ac.uk

MA course in *Writing for Children* available on either a one- or two-year basis. Enquiries: Admissions Officer (☎ 01962 827235).

Greater London

Arvon Foundation
National Administration: 2nd Floor, 42A Buckingham Palace Road, London SW1W 0RE
☎ 020 7931 7611   Fax 020 7963 0961
Website www.arvonfoundation.org

Joint Presidents *Terry Hands, Sir Robin Chichester-Clark*

Devon: Totleigh Barton, Sheepwash, Beaworthy EX21 5NS
☎ 01409 231338   Fax 01409 231144 Email t-barton@arvonfoundation.org
Yorkshire: Lumb Bank, Heptonstall, Hebden Bridge HX7 6DF
☎ 01422 843714   Fax 01422 843714 Email l-bank@arvonfoundation.org
Inverness-shire: Moniack Mhor, Teavarran, Kiltarlity, Beauly IV4 7HT
☎ 01463 741675 Email m-mhor@arvonfoundation.org
Shropshire: The Hurst, Clunton, Craven Arms SY7 0JA
☎ 01588 640658   Fax 01588 640509 Email hurst@arvonfoundation.org
Chairman *Prue Skene, CBE*
National Director *Helen Chaloner*

FOUNDED 1968. Offers people of any age (over 16) and any background the opportunity to live and work with professional writers. Four-and-a-half-day residential courses are held throughout the year at Arvon's four centres, covering poetry, fiction, drama, writing for children, songwriting and the performing arts. Bursaries towards the cost of course fees are available for those on low incomes, the unemployed, students and pensioners. Runs a biennial poetry competition.

The City Literary Institute

Humanities Dept, Stukeley Street, London WC2B 5LJ

☎ 020 7430 0542   Fax 020 7405 3347

Email humanities@citylit.ac.uk

The Writing School offers a wide range of courses from *Ways Into Creative Writing* and *Writing for Children* to *Playwriting* and *Writing Short Stories*. Various lengths of course available. The Department offers information and advice during term time.

London School of Journalism

126 Shirland Road, London W9 2BT

☎ 020 7289 7777   Fax 020 7432 8141

Email info@lsjournalism.com

Website www.home-study.com

Contact *Student Administration Office*

Distance learning courses with an individual and personal approach. Students remain with the same tutor throughout the course. Options include: *Short Story Writing; Writing for Children; Poetry; Freelance Journalism; Media Law; Improve Your English; Cartooning; Thriller Writing*. Fees vary but range from £295 for *Enjoying English Literature* to £395 for *Journalism and Newswriting*. NUJ-recognised Postgraduate Diploma Courses taught in London (three month full-time, six month part-time, nine month evening classes). Online postgraduate diploma course also available.

Greater Manchester

Manchester Metropolitan University – The Writing School

Department of English, Geoffrey Manton Building, Rosamond Street West, off Oxford Road, Manchester M15 6LL

☎0161 247 1732/1   Fax 0161 247 6345

Email m.schmidt@mmu.ac.uk

Course Convenor *Michael Schmidt*

Closely associated with Carcanet Press Ltd and *PN Review*, The Writing School offers four 'routes' for students to follow: *Poetry*, *The Novel*, *Life Writing* and *Writing for Children*. A key feature of the programme is regular readings, lectures, workshops and masterclasses by writers, publishers, producers, booksellers, librarians and agents. Tutors include Simon Armitage, Carol Ann Duffy, Sophie Hannah and Jeffrey Wainwright.

The Writers Bureau

Sevendale House, 7 Dale Street, Manchester M1 1JB

☎0161 228 2362   Fax 0161 236 9440

Email studentservices@writersbureau.com

Website www.writersbureau.com

Comprehensive home-study writing course with personal tuition service from professional writers. Fiction, non-fiction, articles, short stories, novels, TV, radio and drama all covered in detail. Trial period, guarantee and no time limits. Writing for children and biographies, memoirs and family history courses also available. ODLQC accredited. Quote Ref. EH04. Free enquiry line: 0800 856 2008.

Northamptonshire

Knuston Hall Residential College for Adult Education

Irchester, Wellingborough NN29 7EU

☎01933 312104   Fax 01933 357596

Email enquiries@knustonhall.org.uk
Website www.knustonhall.org.uk

Writing courses being held in 2004 included: *Write – and Illustrate a Picture Book for Children; Reminiscence Writing; Telling a Tale; Creative Writing – First Steps; Writing for Children* and *Writing Your Own Murder Mystery.*

Yorkshire

University of Sheffield
Institute for Lifelong Learning, 196–198 West Street, Sheffield S1 4ET
☎ 0114 222 7000   Fax 0114 222 7001
Website www.shef.ac.uk/till

Certificate in *Creative Writing* (Degree Level 1) and a wide range of courses, from foundation level to specialist writing areas, open to all. Courses in poetry, prose, journalism, scriptwriting, comedy, travel writing, writing using ICT/Web, writing for children. Brochures and information available from the address above.

Bursaries and Prizes

Hans Christian Andersen Awards

IBBY, Nonnenweg 12, Postfach, CH-4003 Basel, Switzerland
☎ 00 41 61 272 2917   Fax 00 41 61 272 2757
Email ibby@ibby.org
Website www.ibby.org

Executive Director *Kimete Basha i Novosejt*

The highest international prizes for children's literature: The Hans Christian Andersen Award for Writing, established 1956; The Hans Christian Andersen Award for Illustration, established 1966. Candidates are nominated by National Sections of IBBY (The International Board on Books for Young People). Biennial prizes are awarded, in even-numbered years, to an author and an illustrator whose body of work has made a lasting contribution to children's literature. 2004 winners: Award for Writing: Martin Waddell (Ireland); Award for Illustration: Max Velthuijs (The Netherlands).
AWARD Gold medals.

Angus Book Award

Angus Council Cultural Services, County Buildings, Forfar DD8 3WF
☎ 01307 461460   Fax 01307 462590
Email cultural.services@angus.gov.uk

Contact *Moyra Hood, Educational Resources Librarian*

Established 1995. Designed to try to help teenagers develop an interest in and enthusiasm for reading. Eligible books are read and voted on by third-year schoolchildren in all eight Angus secondary schools. 2003 winner: Keith Gray *Warehouse.*

PRIZE £250 cheque, plus trophy in the form of a replica Pictish stone.

Arts Council Children's Award

Arts Council England, 14 Great Peter Street, London SW1P 3NQ

☎ 020 7333 0100

Website www.artscouncil.org.uk

Contact *Theatre Writing Section*

An annual award for playwrights who write for children. The plays, which must have been produced professionally between 1 July 2004 and 30 June 2005 should be suitable for children up to the age of 12 and be at least 45 minutes long. The playwright must be resident in UK. Closing date for entries: 2 July 2005. Contact the Theatre Writing Section for full details and application form. 2004 winner: Charles Way *Red Red Shoes.*

AWARD £6000.

Bisto/CBI Book of the Year Awards

Children's Books Ireland, 17 Lower Camden Street, Dublin 2, Republic of Ireland

☎ 00 353 1 872 5854   Fax 00 353 1 872 5854

Email bistoawards@childrensbooksireland.com

Contact *Liz Marshall*

FOUNDED 1990 as Bisto Book of the Decade Awards. This led to the establishment of an annual award made by the Irish Children's Book Trust, later to become Children's Books Ireland. Open to any author or illustrator of children's books born or resident in Ireland; open to English or Irish languages. Final entry date 31 January. 2002/03 winners: Marie Louise Fitzpatrick *You, Me and the Big Blue Sea*, Kate Thompson *The Alchemist's*

Apprentice; Patrick Deeley *The Lost Orchard*; Martin Waddell *Ghostly Tales*; Martina Murphy *Dirt Tracks*; Eoin Colfer *The Wish List*.
PRIZES £3000 (Bisto Book of the Year); £1000 (Eilís Dillon Award); three merit awards £800 each.

Blue Peter Book Awards

c/o Awards Administrator, Fraser Ross Associates, 6 Wellington Place, Edinburgh EH6 7EQ
☎0131 553 2759   Fax 0131 553 2759
Email lindsey.fraser@tiscali.co.uk
Website www.bbc.co.uk/bluepeter

Contacts *Lindsey Fraser, Kathryn Ross*

Established in 1999 to highlight paperback fiction, poetry and non-fiction for young people. The initial shortlist is selected by a panel of adults and the final decisions are taken by a panel of Blue Peter judges. Final entry date: mid-June. Previous winners: Nicky Singer *Feather Boy*; Philip Reeve *Mortal Engines*.
AWARD Trophy.

Booktrust Teenage Prize

Book House, 45 East Hill, London SW18 2QZ
☎020 8516 2986   Fax 020 8516 2978
Email hannah@booktrust.org.uk
Website www.bookheads.org.uk

Contact *Hannah Rutland*

Established 1993. Annual prize that recognises a and celebrates the best in teenage fiction. Funded and administered by Booktrust. Open to works of fiction for young adults in the UK, the books to be published between 1 July 2004 and 30 June 2005. Final entry date in March. 2003 winner: Mark Haddon *The Curious Incident of the Dog in the Night-time*.
PRIZE £1500.

The Branford Boase Award
9 Bolderwood Close, Bishopstoke, Eastleigh so50 8TG
☎ 023 8060 0439
Email anne@marleyhcl.freeserve.co.uk
Website www.henriettabranford.co.uk

Administrator *Anne Marley*

Established in 2000 in memory of children's novelist, Henrietta Branford and editor and publisher, Wendy Boase. To be awarded annually to encourage and celebrate the most promising novel by a new writer of children's books, while at the same time highlighting the importance of the editor in nurturing new talent. 2003 winner: Kevin Brooks *Martyn Pig* (book); Barry Cunningham, **The Chicken House** (editor).
AWARD Specially commissioned box, carved and inlaid in silver with the Branford Boase Award logo.

CILIP: The Chartered Institute of Library and Information Professionals' Carnegie Medal
7 Ridgmount Street, London WC1E 7AE
☎ 020 7255 0650   Fax 020 7255 0501
Website www.ckg.org.uk

Established 1936. Presented for an outstanding book for children written in English and first published in the UK during the preceding year. Fiction, non-fiction and poetry are all eligible. 2002 winner (presented in 2003): Sharon Creech *Ruby Holler*.
AWARD Medal.

CILIP: The Chartered Institute of Library and Information Professionals' Kate Greenaway Medal
7 Ridgmount Street, London WC1E 7AE
☎ 020 7255 0650   Fax 020 7255 0501
Website www.ckg.org.uk

Established 1955. Presented annually for the most distinguished work in the illustration of children's books first published in the UK during the preceding year. 2002 winner (presented in 2003): *Jethro Byrde – Fairy Child* by Bob Graham.

AWARD Medal. The Colin Mears Award (£5000 cash) is given annually to the winner of the Kate Greenaway Medal.

Eleanor Farjeon Award

Children's Book Circle, c/o Hodder Children's Books, 338 Euston Road, London NW1 3BH

☎ 020 7873 6483

This award, named in memory of the much-loved children's writer, is for distinguished services to children's books either in this country or overseas, and may be given to a librarian, teacher, publisher, bookseller, author, artist, reviewer, television producer, etc. Nominations from members of the **Children's Book Circle.** 2003 winner: Miriam Hodgson.

AWARD £750.

The Guardian Children's Fiction Award

The Guardian, 119 Farringdon Road, London EC1R 3ER

☎ 020 7239 9694   Fax 020 7713 4366

Children's Book Editor *Julia Eccleshare*

Established 1967. Annual award for an outstanding work of fiction for children aged seven and over by a British or Commonwealth author, first published in the UK in the year of the award, excluding picture books. Final entry date: 1 June. No application form necessary. 2003 winner: Mark Haddon *The Curious Incident of the Dog in the Night-Time.*

AWARD £1500.

Mary Vaughan Jones Award

Cyngor Llyfrau Cymru (Welsh Books Council), Castell Brychan, Aberystwyth SY23 2JB

☎ 01970 624151   Fax 01970 625385
Email wbc.children@wbc.org.uk
Website www.wbc.org.uk

Contact *The Administrator*

Triennial award for distinguished services in the field of children's litera-
ture in Wales over a considerable period of time. 2003 winner: Elfyn
Pritchard.
AWARD Silver trophy.

Lancashire County Library Children's Book of the Year Award

Lancashire County Library Headquarters, County Hall, PO Box 61,
Preston PR1 8RJ
☎ 01772 534040   Fax 01772 264043
Email jean.wolstenholme@lcl.lancscc.gov.uk

Manager, Young People's Service *Jean Wolstenholme*

Established 1986. Annual award, presented in June for a work of original
fiction suitable for 12–14-year-olds. The winner is chosen by 13–14-year-
old secondary school pupils in Lancashire. Books must have been published between 1 September and 31 August in the previous year of the
award and authors must be UK and Republic of Ireland residents. Final
entry date: 1 September each year. 2003 winner: Julie Bertagna *Exodus*.
PRIZE £500, plus engraved glass decanter.

The Astrid Lindgren Memorial Award for Literature

Swedish National Council for Cultural Affairs, PO Box 8743, SE-103
98 Stockholm Sweden
☎ 00 46 8 519 264 00/08   Fax 00 46 8 519 264 99
Email anna.cokorilo@kulturradet.se
Website www.alma.se

Project Manager *Anna Cokorilo*

Established 2002 by the Swedish government in memory of the children's author Astrid Lindgren. Administered by the Swedish National Council for Cultural Affairs, it is an international award for children's and young people's literature given annually to one or more recipients, irrespective of language or nationality. Writing, illustrating and storytelling, as well as reading promotion activities may be awarded. Selected organisations worldwide will be invited to submit nominations; jury members may also contribute nominations. Inaugural winner: Christine Nostlinger.
AWARD SEK 5 million (approx. £500,000)

Macmillan Prize for a Children's Picture Book Illustration
Macmillan Children's Books, 20 New Wharf Road, London N1 9RR
☎ 020 7014 6124   Fax 020 7014 6142
Email i.blundell@macmillan.co.uk
Website www.panmacmillan.com
Contact *Imogen Blundell, Macmillan Children's Books*

Set up in order to stimulate new work from young illustrators in art schools, and to help them start their professional lives. Fiction or non-fiction. Macmillan have the option to publish any of the prize winners.
PRIZES £1000 (1st); £500 (2nd); £250 (3rd).

Marsh Award for Children's Literature in Translation
National Centre for Research in Children's Literature, University of Surrey Roehampton, Digby Stuart College, Roehampton Lane, London SW15 5PH
☎ 020 8392 3008   Fax 020 8392 3819
Email g.lathey@roehampton.ac.uk
Contact *Dr Gillian Lathey*

Established 1995 and sponsored by the Marsh Christian Trust, the award aims to encourage translation of foreign children's books into English. It is a biennial award (next award: 2005), open to British translators of books for 4–16-year-olds, published in the UK by a British publisher. Any category will be considered with the exception of encyclopedias and reference books. No electronic books. 2003 winner: Anthea Bell for her translation of *Where Were You Robert?* by Hans Magnus Enzensberger. PRIZE £1000.

Nestlé Smarties Book Prize

Booktrust, 45 East Hill, London SW18 2QZ
☎ 020 8516 2977   Fax 020 8516 2978
Email hannah@booktrust.org.uk
Website www.booktrusted.com

Contact *Hannah Rutland*

Established 1985 to encourage high standards and stimulate interest in books for children, this prize is given for a children's book (fiction or poetry), written in English by a citizen of the UK or an author resident in the UK, and published in the UK in the year ending 31 October. There are three age-group categories: 5 and under, 6–8 and 9–11. Uniquely, the shortlist for each age category is judged by classes of schoolchildren, who enter a competition to win a chance to be Young Judges. 50 classes from each age category judge the books, deciding who gets Gold, Silver and Bronze. The class projects entered for the judging process are then judged to see which classes will come to London for the prize presentation. 2003 Gold Award winners: Ursula Jones and Russell Ayto *The Witch's Children and the Queen* (5 and under); S.F. Said *Varjek Paws* (6–8); David Almond *The Fire-Eaters* (9–11); Sally Gardner *The Countess' Calamity* (Kids' Clubs Network Special Award).
PRIZES in each category: £2500 (gold); £1500 (silver); £500 (bronze).

The Red House Children's Book Award

The Federation of Children's Book Groups, The Old Malt House, Aldbourne SN8 2DW
☎ 01672 540629   Fax 01672 541280
Email marianneadey@aol.com

Coordinator *Marianne Adey*

Established 1980. Awarded annually for best book of fiction suitable for children. Unique in that it is judged by the children themselves. 2003 winner: *Skeleton Key* by Anthony Horowitz.

AWARD Portfolio of letters, drawings and comments from the children who took part in the judging. Silver bowls and trophy.

Scottish Arts Council Book Awards

Scottish Arts Council, 12 Manor Place, Edinburgh EH3 7DD

☎ 0131 226 6051   Fax 0131 225 9833

Email gavin.wallace@scottisharts.org.uk

Website www.scottisharts.org.uk

Contact *Gavin Wallace, Literature Officer*

Awards are made annually and are given in recognition of high standards in fiction, poetry, non-fiction and literary non-fiction. Authors should be Scottish or resident in Scotland, but books of Scottish interest by other authors are eligible for consideration. Applications are made by publishers only, and the closing date is 31 January for books published in the previous calendar year.

AWARDS Three shortlisted adult and three shortlisted children's writers each receive an award of £2000. The Scottish Arts Council Book of Year Award is worth a total of £10,000 and the Children's Book of the Year is a total of £5000.

WHSmith's 'People's Choice' Book Awards

WHSmith PLC, Nations House, 103 Wigmore Street, London W1U 1WH

☎ 020 7514 9623   Fax 020 7514 9635

Email elizabeth.walker@WHSmith.co.uk

Website www.WHSmithbookawards.co.uk

Contact *Elizabeth Walker, Group Event Marketing Manager*

Now in their fourth year, these WHSmith book awards were the first where the winners are voted for entirely by the public. Teams of celebrity and public judges choose the shortlists but *any* book published during the calendar year can be voted for. There are nine award categories in total. Eight are voted for by the public: Fiction; Debut Novel; Lifestyle; Autobiography/Biography; Travel Writing; Business; Factual and Teen Choice. Voting (in any WHSmith store, local library, by text message, freepost or via the website) starts in January (lasting six weeks) and winners are announced in March. Recent winners have included Jamie Oliver, Ben Elton, Sir David Attenborough and Donna Tartt. The ninth category, the long-standing WHSmith Literary Award, is not put out to public vote but is decided by a panel led by the Professor of English Literature at Merton College, Oxford, and Chief Book Reviewer for the *Sunday Times*, John Carey. Three members of the public join at shortlist stage to help decide the winner.

PRIZES Each winning author receives a trophy and £5000.

The Tir Na N-Og Award
Cyngor Llyfrau Cymru (Welsh Books Council), Castell Brychan, Aberystwyth SY23 2JB
☎ 01970 624151   Fax 01970 625385
Email wbc.children@wbc.org.uk
Website www.wbc.org.uk

An annual award given to the best original book published for children in the year prior to the announcement. There are three categories: Best Welsh Fiction; Best Welsh Non-fiction; Best English Book with an authentic Welsh background.
AWARDS £1000 (each category).

Whitbread Book Awards
The Booksellers Association, Minster House, 272 Vauxhall Bridge Road, London SW1V 1BA
☎ 020 7802 0802   Fax 020 7802 0803

Email nicola.tarling@booksellers.co.uk
Website www.whitbread-bookawards.co.uk

Contact *Nicola Tarling*

Established 1971. The awards celebrate and promote the best contemporary British writing. They are judged in two stages and offer a total of £50,000 prize money. The awards are open to novel, first novel, biography, poetry and children's book, each judged by a panel of three judges, with two young judges joining the panel for the Whitbread Children's Book Award. The winner of each award receives £5000. The Whitbread Book of the Year (£25,000) is chosen from the category winners. Writers must have lived in Britain and Ireland for three or more years. Submissions received from publishers only. Closing date: early July. Sponsored by Whitbread PLC. 2003 winners: David Almond *The Fire-Eaters* (children's); Mark Haddon *The Curious Incident of the Dog in the Night-time* (novel & overall winner); D.B.C. Pierre *Vernon God Little* (first novel); D.J. Taylor *Orwell: The Life* (biography); Don Paterson *Landing Light* (poetry).

Youngminds Book Award

Youngminds, 102–108 Clerkenwell Road, London EC1M 5SA
☎ 020 7336 8445   Fax 020 7336 8446
Email bookaward@youngminds.org.uk
Website www.youngminds.org.uk/bookaward

Contacts *Richard Meigr, Tarryn Hawley*

Established 2003. This award is given to a published work of literature that throws fresh light on the ways a child takes in and makes sense of the world he or he is growing into – novels, memoirs, diaries, poetry collections which portray something of the unique subtlety of a child's experience. 2003 winner: Judy Pascoe.

FURTHER READING
Children's Book Prizes by Ruth Allen (Ashgate Publishing, 1998)

Library Services

Barbican Library
Barbican Centre, London EC2Y 8DS
☎ 020 7638 0569   Fax 020 7638 2249
Email barbicanlib@corpoflondon.gov.uk
Website www.cityoflondon.gov.uk/libraries

OPEN 9.30 am to 5.30 pm Monday and Wednesday; 9.30 am to 7.30 pm Tuesday and Thursday; 9.30 am to 2.00 pm Friday; 9.30 am to 4.00 pm Saturday
OPEN ACCESS

Situated on Level 2 of the Barbican Centre, this is the Corporation of London's largest lending library. Study facilities are available plus free Internet access. In addition to a large general lending department, the library seeks to reflect the Centreemphasis on the arts and includes strong collections (including DVDs, videos and CD-ROMs), on painting, sculpture, theatre, cinema and ballet, as well as a large music library with books, scores and CDs (sound recording loans available at a small charge). Also houses the City's main children's library and has special collections on finance, natural resources, conservation, socialism and the history of London. Service available for housebound readers. A literature events programme is organised by the Library which supplements and provides cross-arts planning opportunities with the Barbican Centre artistic programme. Reading groups meet in the library on the first Tuesday and Thursday of every month.

Booktrust Children's Reference Library

Book House, 45 East Hill, London sw18 2QZ

☎ 020 8516 2985   Fax 020 8516 2978

Email ed@booktrust.org.uk

Website www.booktrust.org.uk

Website www.booktrusted.com

Contact *Mr E. Zaghini*

Open 9.00 am to 5.00 pm Monday to Friday (by appointment only)

Access For reference only

A comprehensive collection of children's literature, related books and periodicals. Aims to hold most of all children's titles published within the last two years. An information service covers all aspects of children's literature, including profiles of authors and illustrators. Reading room facilities. Publishes a quarterly magazine, *Booktrust News* and *The Best Book Guide for Children and Young Adults*.